Amillennial (or inaugurated) eschatology strikes a biblical balance between realism and optimism. With clear descriptions, charts, and critiques, Mike Carpenter compares the major eschatological views and demonstrates how amillennialism best harmonizes with covenantal hermeneutics. He then explains the amillennial interpretation of significant scriptural themes such as the last days, the kingdom of God, the one-thousand-year reign of Christ, the battle of Armageddon, and the eternal state. Most importantly, this helpful introduction to amillennialism points the reader to the Christ who reigns in glory over both this age and the age to come.

—**Joel R. Beeke**, Chancellor and Professor of Homiletics & Systematic Theology, Puritan Reformed Theological Seminary

Doctrine is for Joy, Comfort, and Peace! This insightful, informative, and helpful introduction to amillennialism leads the reader not only to a greater understanding of the covenantal hermeneutics involved in Biblical eschatology, but to behold the Risen & Reigning Savior! This book aims to encourage and inform both pastor and pupil. Throughout, Mike's love for Christ, his affection for Holy Scripture, and his commitment to excellent scholarship provide an engaging presentation of an oft neglected series of joys, comforts, and lasting peace!

—**Kevin M. Hass**, Founding Pastor, By Grace Community Church (PCA), Yorktown, VA

Most books on last things are sensational and speculative. Mike Carpenter's book is neither. *The All-Encompassing Return of Christ* is a clear, simple, and rigorously biblical explanation of what the Bible teaches about the end of the world. Read this book to better understand the end times yourself, or to help others who are uncertain about what they believe. Most importantly, read this book to increase your longing for the all-encompassing return of Christ!

—**M. Hopson Boutot**, Lead Pastor, Poquoson Baptist Church, Poquoson, VA

In an age of constant social media speculation and eschatological squabbles, Mike Carpenter's work provides a refreshing overview of the Amillennial perspective. *All-Encompassing Return* is weighty enough for the pastor who is feeding his flock and growing as a theologian, but accessible enough for the layman who has little familiarity with amillennialism. Mike's story of his transition out of dispensationalism puts the reader at ease and his comprehensive approach to the subject matter leaves them well-learned. Doctrinally strong, understandable, and Christ-exalting—this wonderful resource will have you longing for the return of King Jesus.

—**Michael Howard**, Pastor, Seaford Baptist Church, Yorktown, VA

In a world hurdling headlong into destruction and judgment, Christians are privileged to proclaim the good news of Jesus Christ. Unfortunately, the hope of the gospel is often muddled by bogus interpretations of Christ's return. Consequently, what ought to be comforting can become confusing and frightening. How refreshing to have a work like Mike Carpenter's *The All-Encompassing Return of Christ*. Written from the Reformed perspective, Carpenter's introduction provides a thoroughgoing, accessible guide to the proper biblical interpretation of eschatological issues. In dialogue with the various understandings of the end times, he cogently makes the case for amillennialism being the most faithful to the biblical witness. Readers are returned again and again to the fact that the sovereignty of Jesus Christ is indisputable and there will be no doubt when the King of Kings and Lord of Lords returns in his all-encompassing triumph!

—**The Rev. Dr. T. Scott Landrum**, Pastor, St. James Lutheran Church,
Sumter, South Carolina, and author of
Martin Luther's Hidden God:
Toward a Lutheran Apologetic for the Problem of Evil and Divine Hiddenness.

Eschatology and the book of Revelation in particular have always held a unique place in the minds of Christians. Some have had a disproportionate focus on the topic and the book, using it to define their own and others' theology and a basis for whether to unite with other believers. On the other end of the spectrum are those Christians who avoid the topic as much as possible and are possibly intimidated by the prophetic language and imagery. Mike Carpenter makes a serious contribution to our understanding of eschatology. Whether you agree with his particular interpretation or not you need to read this book for several reasons; one, he provides a model for understanding prophetic and eschatological writings; two, he places eschatology in its proper perspective, not a defining mark of a Christian but nothing to avoid; and three, he writes in plain understandable language accessible to all. Do yourself a favor and read this book.

—**Brian Baugus**, Associate Professor, Business, Leadership & Management,
Regent University

THE
ALL-ENCOMPASSING
RETURN
OF CHRIST

AN INTRODUCTION
TO AMILLENNIALISM

MICHAEL
CARPENTER

NASHVILLE

NEW YORK • LONDON • MELBOURNE • VANCOUVER

The All-Encompassing Return of Christ

An Introduction to Amillennialism

Published in New York, New York, by Morgan James Publishing. Morgan James is a trademark of Morgan James, LLC. www.MorganJamesPublishing.com

Proudly distributed by Publishers Group West®

ISBN 9781636983479 paperback
ISBN 9781636983486 ebook
Library of Congress Control Number:
2023949503

Cover & Interior Design by:
Christopher Kirk
www.GFSstudio.com

Builds *with...* **Habitat for Humanity®** Peninsula and Greater Williamsburg

Morgan James is a proud partner of Habitat for Humanity Peninsula and Greater Williamsburg. Partners in building since 2006.

Get involved today! Visit: www.morgan-james-publishing.com/giving-back

For the saints of Reformation Christian Fellowship, Newport News, Virginia

TABLE OF CONTENTS

ACKNOWLEDGMENTS

There are many who helped me begin and complete the process of writing and publishing this book. First, thank you to Kevin Harrison for encouraging me and connecting me with David Hancock and Isaiah Taylor at Morgan James Publishing. Thank you to David and Isaiah for their guidance along the way. Also, thanks to the production and author support teams at Morgan James for their generous assistance.

Thank you to Michael Hamilton, Greg Kurtz, and Dave Mitchell from Good Comma Editing for your diligence in editing. Your suggestions were vital to the process.

Special thanks to the precious saints of Reformation Christian Fellowship (RCF) and my fellow elders Kenneth D'Auria, Steve Simkins, Matthew Carpenter, and James Lipford. The elders and the body encouraged me to publish as books theological courses I have written for RCF. Also, thank you to Emily Cooper from RCF for your helpful review of my manuscript. I love all of you at RCF and am thankful for our walk together in Christ.

Thank you to my lovely wife, Sonya, and our children and grandchildren for their love and support. Finally, thank you to our Lord Jesus Christ for his gracious salvation, his grace for life, and his sure return. Soli Deo Gloria!

PART 1:
AMILLENNIAL FOUNDATIONS

When presenting a case for a particular position on a debatable subject, how the position was formulated is as important as what is presented. The first three chapters present foundational considerations for amillennialism.

Chapter 1

THE GROUND RULES

In October 1982, I moved from my hometown, Hattiesburg, Mississippi, to Las Vegas, Nevada. I was newly commissioned as an Air Force officer and stationed at Nellis Air Force Base near Las Vegas. In God's providence, this move began a season of significant change—much more than a change in location, much more than leaving the humidity of the southeast for the aridness of the southwest, and much more than transitioning from civilian life to military life. My move to Las Vegas proved to be a thorough spiritual renewal.

I grew up in a Christian home and knew nothing other than being actively involved in church. So, when I moved to Las Vegas, I immediately found a new church family. I joined one I had met two years earlier when I was with my father on a mission trip. Even though I quickly became active in my newfound church, I was not growing in my walk with Christ. But over the years I spent in Las Vegas, God used personal trials, depression, and godly friends to wake me from my slumber. Through his Word and his Spirit, he transformed me from one who rarely read the Bible to one who could not get enough of the Bible.

Given my thirst for God's Word, I listened faithfully to the local Christian radio station that broadcast teachings from various pastors and Bible teachers. One of the series aired was an exposition of Revelation. I listened with great interest, and what I heard was fascinating. I had never heard Revelation interpreted in this manner. No secret rapture? No seven-year tribulation? No future millennium? No "partial return" of Christ on the clouds before his final return as a Warrior King? These were all aspects of the second coming of Christ I had been taught in my church back home—ones the radio preacher in Las Vegas proclaimed as incorrect. This preacher presented an alternative to my upbringing. He spoke of one return of Christ that would wrap up the current age and usher in the new heavens and new earth. He taught an all-encompassing return of Christ, which would include believers and unbelievers being resurrected in a single resurrection, a single final judgment, the demise of Satan and all evil, and the ushering in of the final state of the new heavens and new earth. He was teaching Revelation from an amillennial perspective.

Premillennialism, and dispensationalism in general, were all I had ever known, but I had never truly embraced either. My attitude when taught dispensational premillennialism was "Well, if you say so." Before my Las Vegas growth, I hadn't known any different, and I had no interest in seriously studying the Bible. But now, my new desire to study the Scriptures and this new perspective about the end times led me not only out of dispensationalism but also into a covenantal understanding of the Bible and reformed theology. The Air Force eventually moved me from Las Vegas, but I left a different Christian than when I had arrived. My ground rules for approaching the Bible had changed.

Rules of Biblical Interpretation

Ground rules are important. Just as an athletic competition requires an agreed-upon set of rules, biblical interpretation must have the same. Disagreements over what the Bible says can often be traced back to differences in how to approach the Bible. Therefore, before we go further, let's define some terms and establish the method of interpretation.

Terminology

- Eschatology–the study of the last things. The word *eschatology* comes from two Greek words: *eschatos* and *logos*. *Eschatos* means "last," and *logos* means "word or speech"; therefore, eschatology literally is a word or speech about the last things. The field of eschatology encompasses more than the second coming of Christ, but it includes the second coming of Christ.
- Millennium–one thousand years. In biblical eschatology, the millennium refers to the one thousand years found in Revelation 20.
- Amillennialism–the position that the one thousand years of Revelation 20 represent the time between the first advent of Christ and the second advent of Christ. Thus, the millennium is not exactly one thousand years and does not begin in the future. Since the millennium spans the period between the cross and the return of Christ, Christ will return after the millennium.

- Premillennialism–the position that the one thousand years of Revelation 20 will occur in the future and will be exactly one thousand years.[1] The *pre-* prefix indicates Christ will return before the millennium begins.

- Postmillennialism–the position that the one thousand years of Revelation 20 will occur in the future and may or may not be exactly one thousand years. The *post-* prefix indicates Christ will return after the millennium.

- Dispensationalism–the position that the history of redemption is revealed through dispensations. A dispensation is a period of history when God related (or will relate) to man differently. Since a dispensation is based on a change in how God is working in redemptive history, dispensations cannot overlap.

- Covenantalism–the position that the history of redemption is revealed through covenants that show the unity of the people of God across all history. Covenants overlap because there is one redemptive plan, and the covenants are fulfilled in Christ in the New Covenant.

These are broad definitions that I will clarify as we proceed, and I will define other terms as needed.

Hermeneutics

Second, let's consider hermeneutics. Hermeneutics are the collection of principles we use to interpret Scripture. While this is not a book on principles for interpreting the Bible, we need a few ground rules for biblical hermeneutics because much disagreement over what the Bible means is due to prevailing principles of interpretation. Many who read the Bible fail to consider what principles to use when interpreting Scripture. Without saying it, many adhere to the principle that "The Bible means whatever I think it means." We want to avoid this approach to interpreting the Bible.

I subscribe to three major principles of interpretation. The primary principle is *Scripture interprets Scripture* (also known as the analogy of faith). First and foremost, we should use the Bible to interpret the Bible. Positively, this means other passages of Scripture help us understand the passage we are studying. Negatively, this means no interpretation of a

---

1 Most premillennialists believe the millennium will span one thousand years, but there are some historic premillennialists who do not take the one thousand years of Revelation 20 to be literal.

portion of Scripture can conflict with what is clearly taught in other portions of Scripture. There are some corollaries to the analogy of faith.

- Interpret the Old Testament in light of the New Testament.
- Interpret the unclear in light of the clear.
- Interpret the implicit in light of the explicit.

The second major principle for interpreting the Bible is *interpret according to the literal sense.* Interpreting according to the literal sense does not mean interpreting the Bible in a strictly literal manner that ignores the normal rules of literature. It means we interpret according to the normal rules of grammar, speech, syntax, genre, and context. This principle restrains us from speculation, and it requires we know the literary genres and forms of Scripture (narrative, poetry, etc.).

The final major principle is *interpret considering the grammar and history of the text* (often called grammatical-historical interpretation). This principle is closely related to the literal-sense principle and focuses on the grammatical constructs and historical contexts of Scripture. Grammatical structure determines whether a specific passage should be considered a question (interrogative), command (imperative), or declaration (indicative). It seeks to understand the original meaning of the text to prevent us from reading into Scripture our thoughts from the present.

There are certainly other important factors to consider when interpreting the Bible (i.e., considering narrative passages in light of declarative passages), but these three overarching principles are the most foundational.

Does everyone who prioritizes these principles agree with my conclusions about the end times? No. These principles are vital, but even those who use these principles may still disagree with my position on eschatology. This disagreement doesn't invalidate the three principles. It simply demonstrates our fallibility. While I am confident in my interpretation of the end times, I cannot be prideful. None of us are infallible interpreters of Scripture.

Eschatological Rules of Interpretation

Now that we have established the rules for biblical interpretation, let's narrow the focus to eschatology. During my time of growth in Las Vegas, that radio Bible teacher made three points in his lectures about the book of Revelation that transformed my thinking about eschatology:

- Revelation must be interpreted according to its genre.
- Revelation must make sense to the original recipients.
- The Church is the true Israel.

As I continued to study, I came to realize these three issues are critical in how one understands not only the millennium but all of eschatology. Other important issues exist, but these three moved to the forefront for me. In fact, if you and I disagree on these points, I doubt we will see eye to eye when it comes to many of the aspects of the return of Christ. We can certainly agree Christ will return to "judge the living and the dead" (2 Timothy 4:1), but we will diverge on the details. To be clear, my primary goal is not agreement but understanding. Yes, I hope this book will encourage many to study amillennialism further, but I also desire this introduction to amillennialism will bring understanding where confusion often reigns.

The first two of the above items relate to the New Testament book of Revelation. This book is not a study of Revelation, but no look at the return of Christ can ignore the last book of the New Testament. The millennium is in Revelation, so how we interpret Revelation impacts how we understand the millennium.

The third item—the Church is the true Israel—is important to eschatology because dispensationalists believe the millennium is a time when God resumes his plan for Israel. However, the relationship between Israel and the Church transcends eschatology.

Respect the Genre

First, when studying Revelation, we must respect the genre. This relates directly to the second principle of interpretation: Interpret according to the literal sense, which includes considering the genre. Fortunately, there is no need to guess the genre of Revelation since the author declares it from the start. The first verses identify Revelation both as "apocalypse" (or "revelation," 1:1) and as prophecy (1:3). (See also 10:11; 22:7, 9, 10, 18, 19.)

"Apocalypse" is derived from the Greek noun *apokalypsis*, meaning "revelation, disclosure, unveiling"—that is, the disclosure of unseen heavenly or future realities. Revelation, therefore, is in the same category as New Testament texts as Jesus's Olivet Discourse (Matthew 24–25) and Paul's discussion of the man of lawlessness (2 Thessalonians 2).[2] Furthermore, the first verse of Revelation says, "He made it known by sending his angel." The KJV translates this phrase as "He sent and signified it by his angel." "Made it known" (ESV) and "signified" (KJV) translate the Greek word *semaino*, which is related to the noun *sema* (*sign*). It means, "to give a sign, signify, indicate" or "make known, report, communicate." Signs point us to reality but are not the reality. A sign that says, "New York City" is not the city of New York but is pointing us to or reminding us of New York City.

---

2   "Introduction to The Revelation to John," *The ESV Study Bible* (Wheaton, IL: Crossway, 2008), 2453–54.

This means we shouldn't take the signs in Revelation literally, but we should see the reality behind the signs. Revelation uses symbolism from beginning to end. However, we can't abandon our hermeneutics and arbitrarily decide what the signs and symbols mean. We must hold fast to the principle, Scripture interprets Scripture. Every chapter has allusions to the Old and New Testaments; thus, we have the whole of Scripture to guide us in our interpretation.

Respect the Audience

Second, when studying Revelation, we must respect the audience. The book of Revelation has the general form of an epistle (letter). There is a greeting (1:4–5b), and it is written to seven historical churches. Therefore, it is an apocalyptic prophecy written in the form of a letter.[3] Revelation was written in the latter part of the first century, and this was a time of persecution. Christians were under attack. John says in Revelation 1:9 that he is on the island of Patmos "on account of the word of God and the testimony of Jesus." He was exiled because he had been preaching Christ. Chapters 2 and 3 contain the letters to the seven churches, and, in each letter, Jesus makes a promise "to the one who conquers" (or overcomes). In the fifth seal in chapter 6, John "saw under the altar the souls of those who had been slain for the word of God and for the witness they had borne" (Revelation 6:9). Chapter 12 describes the persecution of the Church like this:

> And they have conquered him by the blood of the Lamb and by the word
> of their testimony, for they loved not their lives even unto death.
> (Revelation 12:11)

Then we read in verse 17,

> Then the dragon became furious with the woman and went off to make
> war on the rest of her offspring, on those who keep the commandments
> of God and hold to the testimony of Jesus. And he stood on the sand
> of the sea.

Finally, Revelation 20:4 addresses the present reality for the first-century readers, not a future persecution:

---

3   G. K. Beale, *The Book of Revelation*, The New International Greek Testament Commentary (Grand Rapids, MI: Wm. B. Eerdmans Publishing Company, 1999, 2013), 186.

> The souls of those who had been beheaded for the testimony of Jesus and for the word of God, and those who had not worshiped the beast or its image and had not received its mark on their foreheads or their hands.

Revelation would bring much less comfort to the persecuted believers if most of the book is set in the far future. Futurism is an interpretive method that assigns chapters 4–22 to the future—a very distant future from the original recipients.

The opposite end of the interpretive spectrum is preterism. Preterism believes all or most of the prophecies concerning the return of Christ were fulfilled in the first century, by AD 70. Full preterism is not considered orthodox (within the realm of acceptable Christian doctrine) since it denies the future return of Christ, while partial preterism is orthodox because it affirms the future, visible, personal return of Christ. Looking at Revelation through the lens of preterism certainly makes Revelation applicable to the seven churches, but it has less value for those of us far removed from the first century.

Historicism views chapters 4–22 as describing historical events from the early church up to and including the new heavens and new earth. However, the problem with historicism is determining what historical events are revealed.

What we need is a way of interpreting Revelation that is meaningful to the early church and to every generation that follows. Also, we need a method of interpretation that relies on the sixty-five books that precede Revelation in the canon of Scripture. That method is idealism.

Idealism holds to an ongoing conflict between Christ and Satan, which is seen in the conflict of the Church with the world and the evil realm. Apart from events related to the first or second coming of Christ, particular historical events are not described. Instead, Revelation describes the type of events each generation of believers can expect. The conflict that characterizes the gospel age will intensify shortly before Christ returns, but his return will eliminate all evil. Believers under persecution in the seven churches and all believers that are persecuted until Jesus returns see the throne room of God described in Revelation 4–5 and are comforted that he rules over all things, including their trials.

Respect the Unity of God's People

The last truth—one that transformed my thinking—is the Church is the true Israel. (Many would not call this a truth but rather a serious error.) This is important because how one understands the relationship between Israel and the Church is tied to how one understands the relationship between the Old Testament and the New Testament. Also, it is tightly tied to the purpose of Christ's first coming and what he accomplished. Which Old Testament promises and prophecies did Christ fulfill in his first advent? The corollary hermeneutical principle, to interpret the Old Testament in light of the New Testament, guides us in answering that question.

The New Testament presents Christ as the fulfillment of all that God has promised. Look at 2 Corinthians 1:19–20:

> For the Son of God, Jesus Christ, whom we proclaimed among you, Silvanus and Timothy and I, was not Yes and No, but in him it is always Yes. *For all the promises of God find their Yes in him.* That is why it is through him that we utter our Amen to God for his glory.

Paul did not say, "For *most of* the promises of God find their Yes in him." No, he said *all* of God's plans and purposes for redemption are wrapped up in Christ. The argument, "But there are promises to Israel unfulfilled," does not withstand the teaching of the New Testament. Jesus said in John 15:1, "I am the true vine." If Jesus is the true vine, who is the false vine? In Isaiah 5:1–7, Judah is presented as the vineyard of the Lord, but this vineyard only produced wild grapes. Because of this the vineyard will be trampled and destroyed. Verse 7 says,

> For the vineyard of the LORD of hosts
>   is the house of Israel,
> and the men of Judah
>   are his pleasant planting;
> and he looked for justice,
>   but behold, bloodshed;
> for righteousness,
>   but behold, an outcry!

Furthermore, Jeremiah writes this of Judah,

> Yet I planted you a choice vine,
>   wholly of pure seed.
> How then have you turned degenerate
>   and become a wild vine? (Jeremiah 2:21)

In these verses, the nation of Israel is presented as the false vine. However, God also promised to restore his vineyard (Isaiah 27:2–6). But how? Through Christ. Thus, when Jesus says he is the true vine, he is proclaiming he is the true Israel. Jesus is the true first-born Son of God (Exodus 4:22; Colossians 1:15; Hebrews 1:6). All of God's people now find their identity in Christ.

What about Jews today, though? If all God's promises to Israel are now fulfilled in Christ and his church, what is left for them? Have they been shortchanged? Never. Paul expresses it this way:

> I ask, then, has God rejected his people? By no means! For I myself am an Israelite, a descendant of Abraham, a member of the tribe of Benjamin. God has not rejected his people whom he foreknew. (Romans 11:1–2a)

God has not rejected the Jewish people. Paul is proof of that. The people of Israel are now offered Christ through the gospel, and "all Israel will be saved" (Romans 8:26). For this reason, we should not tell Jewish people that one day God will fulfill his promises to them in a future millennium. Instead, we should tell them he has fulfilled his promises to them in Christ.

There is no need to wait for God to reinitiate his plan for the Jews. Christ is the only plan for Jews and Gentiles. As Paul said in Romans 10:1 concerning his fellow Israelites, "Brothers, my heart's desire and prayer to God for them is that *they may be saved*." It is interesting that in Paul's longest passage about Israel (Romans 9–11) he focuses on salvation in Christ, not on a future plan for Israel.

Paul's focus is on the Church because the Church is the full realization of the people of God and will be for all eternity. Paul's doxology in Ephesians 3 states this:

> Now to him who is able to do far more abundantly than all that we ask or think, according to the power at work within us, to him be glory in the church and in Christ Jesus throughout all generations, forever and ever. Amen. (Ephesians 3:20–21)

Notice Paul ascribes glory to God in the church and in Christ Jesus. This glory is an eternal glory. Since Paul writes this glory extends "throughout all generations," you could argue that God's glory in the Church is just until Jesus returns. However, he adds "forever and ever," which takes us well past the return of Christ. The Church is God's eternal plan, not a plan B or a parenthesis while he puts his purposes for Israel on hold.

The Church being one with the Old Testament saints is not unique to amillennialism and is not even tied directly to the second coming of Christ. However, God's plan for the Church being distinct from God's plan for Israel is a key tenet of dispensationalism—and drives much of the eschatology of premillennialism. Thus, if the Church and Israel are one people of God, then much of the basis for dispensational premillennialism unravels.

Covenantalism

Earlier I mentioned my transition from dispensationalism to covenantalism (also called Covenant Theology). Covenant Theology views redemptive history from the perspective of the covenants revealed in Scripture and sees unity across redemptive history. The covenants revealed in the Bible are

1. The Covenant of Redemption—established among the persons of the Trinity to accomplish redemption. This covenant is the basis for the trinitarian nature of salvation.

2. The Covenant of Works—established with Adam in the Garden of Eden. Adam's obedience would ensure righteousness and life for him and all his progeny. Adam's disobedience would ensure sin and death for all his progeny.

3. The Covenant of Grace—established after Adam sinned to provide redemption to fallen humanity. This covenant undergirds all the remaining covenants.

4. The Covenant with Noah—established with Noah and his descendants that God will not destroy the earth again by water. This is not a redemptive covenant but serves redemption through God's common grace toward man.

5. The Abrahamic Covenant—established with Abraham. This covenant promises that the offspring of Abraham will bless the nations.

6. The Mosaic (or Old) Covenant—established with Israel after leaving Egypt. This covenant prescribes laws for obedience, sacrifice for atonement, and priests for intercession.

7. The Davidic Covenant—established with David. God promises to build David a forever kingdom, and David's son will rule over this kingdom.

8. The New Covenant—the fulfillment by Christ of all the covenants. Jesus fulfills the Covenant of Works as the obedient last Adam (1 Corinthians 15:45). He is the seed of the woman who bruised the head of the serpent (Genesis 3:15) as promised in the Covenant of Grace. In fulfillment of the Abrahamic Covenant, Jesus is the offspring of Abraham who blesses all the nations, and through Jesus, we are Abraham's offspring (Galatians 3:15–29). Jesus fulfilled all aspects of the Mosaic Covenant. He satisfied the requirements of the law (Matthew 5:17),

accomplished atonement (Hebrews 9:26), and is our great high priest (Hebrews 8:1). He is the Son of David who sits on David's throne (Acts 2:29–36). All of God's promises are "Yes" in him (2 Corinthians 1:20).

There are differences among covenant theologians regarding the number of covenants and the level of continuity between some of the covenants established in the Old Testament and the New Covenant. But a unifying factor is all previous covenants are fulfilled in Christ. There is one people of God because all God's people are in Christ. The Old Testament expression of God's people was Israel, and the New Testament expression of God's people is the Church. All the Old Testament was leading to and pointing to Christ (Luke 24:27; John 5:46).

Dispensationalism

Another primary theological perspective is dispensationalism. It has its roots in the theology of John Nelson Darby. In the early nineteenth century, Darby was an Anglican who left the Church of England and associated with the Plymouth Brethren, a nondenominational group formed by those who had left established denominations. He didn't fully develop dispensationalism, but his ideas about the rapture, tribulation, millennium, and the different histories of Israel and the Church were foundational for the development of dispensational theology. Darby traveled to the United States, where his theology was eventually picked up by C. I. Scofield who went on to publish the Scofield Reference Bible in 1909. That Bible was the most important tool in spreading dispensationalism. Also, dispensational schools emerged and helped to spread this theology.[4]

The key concept in dispensationalism is seeing biblical history as defined by different eras. Charles Ryrie, a prominent twentieth-century dispensationalist, gives this description of dispensationalism:

> Dispensationalism views the world as a household run by God. In this household-world God is dispensing or administering its affairs according to His own will and in various stages of revelation in the process of time. These various stages mark off the distinguishably different economies in the outworking of His total purpose, and these economies are the dispensations.[5]

---

4   Cornelis P. Venema, *The Promise of the Future* (Carlisle, PA: Banner of Truth Trust, 2000), 206–7.

5   Charles C. Ryrie, *Dispensationalism Today* (Chicago: Moody Press, 1965), 31.

Just as you may run your household differently from the way I run my household, dispensationalism says God has run his household, that is the world, in different ways throughout different parts of history. A dispensation, then, marks a period in which God administered his redemptive plan in a way different from other periods of time. Dispensationalism does not ignore the biblical covenants, but the covenants are secondary to the dispensations and are often interpreted in light of them. Just like covenantalists are not unified in their understanding of the covenants, dispensationalists are not unified in their understanding of the dispensations. There are two general categories of dispensationalism: classic and progressive.

Classic Dispensationalism

One of the core beliefs of classic dispensationalism is the separation between Israel and the Church. God has two plans—one for the Church and one for the nation of Israel. This is important because dispensationalists believe God will resume his plan for Israel during the millennium. Traditionally classic dispensationalism has divided biblical history into seven dispensations.

1. The Dispensation of Innocency or Freedom (before the Fall)
2. The Dispensation of Conscience or Self-Determination (after the Fall until the Flood)
3. The Dispensation of Civil Government (after the Flood until Abraham)
4. The Dispensation of Promise or Patriarchal Rule (Abraham until Moses)
5. The Dispensation of Mosaic Law (Moses until Jesus's first coming)
6. The Dispensation of Grace (Jesus's first coming until Jesus's second coming)
7. The Dispensation of the Millennium (Jesus's second coming until the final judgment) [6]

Progressive Dispensationalism

Today, many dispensationalists, especially in academia, are progressive dispensationalists. As with classic dispensationalists, they see a separation between the Church and Israel, and God fulfilling his promises to Israel during the millennium, but ultimately all the people of God, Jews and Gentiles, will share in the same blessings. Progressive dispensationalism also has seven dispensations, but they differ in how they are named, and the final dispensation has no end. The final dispensation begins with the millennium and continues into eternity.

1. The Dispensation of Creation: At Home in the Garden (before the Fall)
2. The Dispensation of the Fall: Exiled from the Garden (after the Fall until the Flood)

---

6   Ryrie, *Dispensationalism Today*, 57–64.

3. The Dispensation of after the Flood: The Rise of Nations (after the Flood until Abraham)

4. The Dispensation of the call of Abraham: Blessing of All Nations (Abraham until Moses)

5. The Dispensation of the Exodus: The Giving of the Law (Moses until Jesus's first coming)

6. The Dispensation of the Spirit: Blessing of All Nations (Jesus's first coming until Jesus's second coming)

7. The Dispensation of the New Heavens and Earth: Redemption Completed (Millennium, final judgment, new heavens and earth)[7]

Summary

Now that we have set the ground rules, we can begin. We have established some definitions along with principles of biblical interpretation.

- Interpret Scripture with Scripture
    - Interpret the Old Testament in light of the New Testament
    - Interpret the unclear in light of the clear
    - Interpret the implicit in light of the explicit
- Interpret according to the literal sense
- Interpret considering the grammar and history of the text

Also, we considered some rules for interpreting eschatology.

- Respect the genre of Revelation (apocalyptic)
- Respect the original audience of Revelation (persecuted believers)
- Respect the unity of God's people (the Church is the true Israel)

Finally, we contrasted a covenantal approach to the Scriptures with a dispensational approach. As we look at each aspect of the return of Christ, we will carry forward what we established here. This is the foundation for our continued study.

---

7   Glenn R. Kreider, "What Is Dispensationalism? A Proposal," in *Dispensationalism and the History of Redemption*, eds. D. Jeffrey Bingham and Glenn R. Kreider (Chicago: Moody Publishers, 2015), 28–36.

My goal is to present an introduction to amillennialism. The key premise of amillennialism is Christ returns once and only once at the end of the age. There are events associated with the second coming of Christ.

1. Just prior to the second advent, there will be great tribulation for the Church. Jesus returns when the situation is most dire for the Church.
2. At his return, all the dead are raised, judgment occurs, Satan along with unbelievers and all evil are cast into the lake of fire (hell), and believers, in their resurrected bodies, live forever with Christ in the New Jerusalem on the new earth (heaven).

All of history is wrapped up when the last trumpet sounds. This is why the return of Christ is all-encompassing.

Chapter 2

THE LAST DAYS AND AGE TO COME

O ne of the challenges of theological study is clarifying terms. More important, however, is knowing that a careful examination of the Scriptures is how to clarify anything related to theology. How the Bible references a particular word or concept must guide our study.

Therefore, before we study the return of Christ, we need to consider the last days. In order to properly interpret the Scriptures concerning the last things, we need to understand how the Scriptures present the last days.

The Bible refers to the last days using a variety of wording: the last days, the last day, the day, the day of the Lord, the age to come, the end of the age, and the latter days. Do all these time references refer to the same period? Let's look at some examples.

First, 2 Timothy 3:1 gives us a clear reference to "the last days":

> But understand this, that in the last days there will come times of difficulty.

In John 6:44 we find "the last day":

> No one can come to me unless the Father who sent me draws him. And I will raise him up on the last day.

Hebrews 10:24–25 speaks of "the day":

> And let us consider how to stir up one another to love and good works, not neglecting to meet together, as is the habit of some, but encouraging one another, and all the more as you see the Day drawing near.

The phrase "the day of the Lord" is found in both the Old and New Testaments. Look at Isaiah 13:6 and 1 Thessalonians 5:2:

> Wail, for the day of the LORD is near; as destruction from the Almighty it will come! (Isaiah 13:6)
> For you yourselves are fully aware that the day of the Lord will come like a thief in the night. (1 Thessalonians 5:2)

In Matthew 12:32 we have "the age to come":

> And whoever speaks a word against the Son of Man will be forgiven, but whoever speaks against the Holy Spirit will not be forgiven, either in this age or in the age to come.

Jesus references "the end of the age" in Matthew 24:3:

> As he sat on the Mount of Olives, the disciples came to him privately, saying, "Tell us, when will these things be, and what will be the sign of your coming and of the end of the age?"

Finally, in the Old Testament, we find the expression "latter days," such as in Isaiah 2:2:

> It shall come to pass in the latter days
>   that the mountain of the house of the LORD
> shall be established as the highest of the mountains,
>   and shall be lifted up above the hills;
> and all the nations shall flow to it.

How do we make sense of all this? Briefly, "the last day," "the day," and "the Day of the Lord" all refer to the time and events associated with Christ's return, specifically the judgment of the wicked. "The age to come," "the end of the age," and "the latter days" all refer to the time period associated with the coming of the Messiah, which overlaps with "this age." With this in mind, there are two questions we will consider: When are the last days, and what does the Bible mean when it refers to "this age" and "the age to come"?

The Last Days

A biblical understanding of the last days is important. Some believe when the Bible speaks of the last days it is referring to the period of time just before the return of Christ. If this is true, then many New Testament passages that speak of the last days would apply only to the final generation of believers. However, such an interpretation falls apart when we allow Scripture to interpret Scripture. When we interpret Scripture with Scripture, we find the "last days" are a much longer period. The last days include the time between the first coming and the second coming of Christ. Thus, in a sense, all of the New Testament is eschatological (all of the New Testament is concerned with the end).

Five New Testament passages in the ESV use the phrase "last days." Let's look at each.

Acts 2:17

Acts 2 tells of the coming of the Holy Spirit on the day of Pentecost when tongues of fire appeared and those waiting in the upper room were filled with the Holy Spirit and began speaking in foreign languages. The people were amazed, but some claimed those filled with the Spirit were drunk. Peter stood up and began preaching. He let the crowd know that neither he nor the others were drunk, but what the crowd was seeing and hearing was the fulfillment of a prophecy spoken by the prophet Joel. In Acts 2:17–21 Peter quoted from the prophet Joel:

> And in the last days it shall be, God declares,
>> that I will pour out my Spirit on all flesh,
> and your sons and your daughters shall prophesy,
>> and your young men shall see visions,
>> and your old men shall dream dreams;
> even on my male servants and female servants
>> in those days I will pour out my Spirit, and they shall prophesy.
> And I will show wonders in the heavens above
>> and signs on the earth below,
>> blood, and fire, and vapor of smoke;
>> the sun shall be turned to darkness
>> and the moon to blood,
>> before the day of the Lord comes, the great and magnificent day.

And it shall come to pass that everyone who calls upon the name of the Lord shall be saved.

Peter took this quote from Joel 2:28–32. Verse 28, in particular, says,

And it shall come to pass afterward,
that I will pour out my Spirit on all flesh;
your sons and your daughters shall prophesy,
your old men shall dream dreams,
and your young men shall see visions.

Notice Joel uses the time reference "afterward." The Lord is promising that after a period of judgment against his people, he will bestow his Spirit on all people. Inspired by the Holy Spirit, Peter proclaimed Pentecost as the beginning of those "afterward" days, what Peter calls "the last days." The last days have continued into the present. These are the last days because the Lord has fulfilled what he promised his people; they would be blessed with the Holy Spirit. So, from our perspective, the last days began over two thousand years ago.

2 Timothy 3:1

Next, let's consider 2 Timothy 3:1–5:

But understand this, that in the last days there will come times of difficulty. For people will be lovers of self, lovers of money, proud, arrogant, abusive, disobedient to their parents, ungrateful, unholy, heartless, unappeasable, slanderous, without self-control, brutal, not loving good, treacherous, reckless, swollen with conceit, lovers of pleasure rather than lovers of God, having the appearance of godliness, but denying its power. Avoid such people.

This passage is often quoted by those who believe the last days are primarily the days just before Christ returns. You will hear them say the return of Jesus is just around the corner; after all, this passage describes what our world looks like more and more. Our nations, cities, and neighborhoods are filled with ungodly people—and things are only getting worse. Surely, they say, this is a sign that we are in the last days.

Well, the decline of our world is a sign we are in the last days but notice the end of verse 5. Paul tells Timothy, "Avoid such people." If Paul is concerned only about the time just prior to the return of Christ, why would he tell Timothy to avoid these kinds of people in the first century? Paul knew the people he described are not limited to the very end. Timothy needed to know there will always be people who are hostile to the gospel. There will always be people who scoff at God's law and promises. This is a sign we are in the last days, but the last days began a long time ago.

Hebrews 1:1-2

The first two verses of Hebrews also clearly show the last days began with Pentecost:

> Long ago, at many times and in many ways, God spoke to our fathers by the prophets, but in these last days he has spoken to us by his Son, whom he appointed the heir of all things, through whom also he created the world.

In the Old Testament, God spoke to His people in many ways and through many different prophets. Pay close attention to what characterizes "these last days." In the last days, God spoke through his Son. We are living in the last days because God has sent his Son. God's final word comes through Jesus. Therefore, the coming of Jesus began the last days.

James 5:3

James 5 references the last days:

> Come now, you rich, weep and howl for the miseries that are coming upon you. Your riches have rotted and your garments are moth-eaten. Your gold and silver have corroded, and their corrosion will be evidence against you and will eat your flesh like fire. You have laid up treasure in the last days. (James 5:1–3)

James condemned the rich who are hoarding earthly wealth. Instead of laying up treasure in heaven during the last days, they were treasuring things that have no lasting value, things that will perish. This warning applied when James wrote his letter, and it still applies today. James, along with the other New Testament writers, understood he was living in the last days.

2 Peter 3:3

Finally, let's consider 2 Peter 3:1–4:

> This is now the second letter that I am writing to you, beloved. In both of them I am stirring up your sincere mind by way of reminder, that you should remember the predictions of the holy prophets and the commandment of the Lord and Savior through your apostles, knowing this first of all, that scoffers will come in the last days with scoffing, following their own sinful desires. They will say, "Where is the promise of his coming? For ever since the fathers fell asleep, all things are continuing as they were from the beginning of creation."

In this passage, Peter addressed those who said Jesus would not return. Scoffers will exist in the last days. As with 2 Timothy 3:1, some try to limit Peter's reference to the last days to the days just before the return of Jesus. But Peter warned the recipients of his letter to beware of those who are skeptical about Jesus's promise to return.

We know from Scripture, from history, and from experience that, ever since Jesus promised he would return, there have been those who have doubted that Jesus would fulfill that promise. Scoffers still abound.

Conclusion

What we find in all these passages is the arrival of Jesus inaugurating the final phase of redemptive history. During these last days, we have the work of the Holy Spirit (Acts 2:17), God has spoken his final word through his Son (Hebrews 1:2), there will be all kinds of ungodliness (2 Timothy 3:1–5), there will be those who strive to gain earthly treasures (James 5:3), and there will always be those who question the return of Christ and the final judgment (2 Peter 3:1–4).

We will discuss this more when we study the second coming of Christ but, realize this: Even though the last days cover the period from the first coming to the second coming of Christ, there is also an expectation of the imminent return of Christ throughout the last days. James 5:8 says, "The coming of the Lord is at hand," and verse 9 says, "The Judge is standing at the door." In Romans 13:11, it is written that our "salvation is nearer to us now than when we first believed." Paul, in Philippians 4:5, says, "The Lord is at hand," and Peter says in 1 Peter 4:7, "The end of all things is at hand." Therefore, in these last days, we are always to eagerly expect the return of Christ.

The Age to Come

In addition to "the last days," there is also "the age to come," which is contrasted with the present age in Matthew 12:32:

> And whoever speaks a word against the Son of Man will be forgiven, but whoever speaks against the Holy Spirit will not be forgiven, either in *this age* or in *the age to come*.

This verse gives us two time periods: this age and the age to come. Mark 10:29–30 also mentions these two ages:

> Jesus said, "Truly, I say to you, there is no one who has left house or brothers or sisters or mother or father or children or lands, for my sake and for the gospel, who will not receive a hundredfold now in *this time*, houses and brothers and sisters and mothers and children and lands, with persecutions, and in *the age to come* eternal life."

However, these two different ages are not just in the New Testament. They originate in the Old Testament. The great expectation of the Old Testament saints was the arrival of the Messiah. The time before the Messiah was a time of trouble and eventually exile, but the exile was not the end of the story. Whenever God proclaimed judgment against his people, he also proclaimed restoration (for example, Jeremiah 29:10–14). The Jews that returned from exile saw a partial fulfillment of God's restoration promise. The ultimate fulfillment would be realized in the coming of Messiah. Even the Samaritan woman at the well said to Jesus, "I know that Messiah is coming (he who is called Christ). When he comes, he will tell us all things" (John 4:25). All will be well because the old age will have been replaced with the age of the Messiah (the age to come).

The New Testament modifies the two-age framework found in the Old Testament. The coming of the Messiah (Jesus) did usher in "the age to come," but it did not end "this age." There is an overlap between the two ages. In other words, this present age and the age to come overlap during the time between the first and second comings of Christ. The current age will end and the latter days, or the "age to come," will arrive in fullness at the consummation of all things when Christ returns.

This is why Jesus taught that the kingdom of God is like a mustard seed that begins small and grows into the largest plant in the garden (Matthew 13:31). It is why, although the new creation has begun in Jesus and our hearts (2 Corinthians 5:17), we still await its fullness at the return of Christ (Revelation 21:1–3). With Christ's first coming, many dimensions of the latter days became reality, but when Christ returns, we will experience them in full measure.[8]

This diagram shows the difference between the perspective of the Old Testament and the perspective of the New Testament:[9]

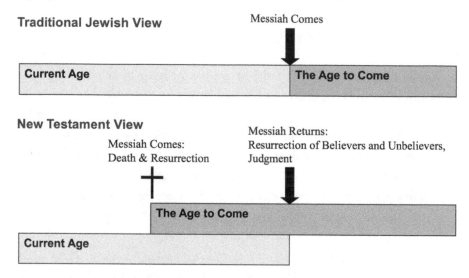

The Old Testament proclaims the golden age begins when the Messiah arrives. However, the New Testament shows there is an overlap between the current age and the age to come. Kim Riddlebarger explains it like this:

> [The time between Christ's resurrection and his return] is marked by the presence of the age to come in some provisional but not fully consummated sense. For example, the presence of the Kingdom of God and the gift of the Holy Spirit are pledges and guarantees of the glorious blessings of the age to come, which will be the inheritance of believers. Christians live in the eschatological tension during the partial overlap of the two ages as they await the arrival of the age to come in its fullness.[10]

---

8   "The Plan of the Ages: Are We in the Last Days?" *The Spirit of the Reformation Study Bible*, ed. Richard L. Pratt Jr. (Grand Rapids, MI: Zondervan, 2003), 1988–89.

9   Adapted from "The Plan of the Ages," *The Spirit of the Reformation Study Bible*, 1989.

10 Kim Riddlebarger, *A Case for Amillennialism* (Grand Rapids, MI: Baker Books, 2013), 103. Excerpt from *A Case for Amillennialism* by Kim Riddlebarger, copyright © 2013. Used by permission of Baker Books, a division of Baker Publishing Group.

This perspective is taught by both Jesus and Paul. This age consists of things that are temporary because they pass away when Christ returns. The age to come consists of things eternal. Riddlebarger gives a helpful summary of each age.[11]

The Temporal Characterizes the Current Age

- Matthew 12:32–There is no forgiveness for blasphemy against the Holy Spirit.
- Matthew 24:3–The end of the age will be preceded by signs.
- Matthew 28:20–Christ will be with us until the end of the age.
- Mark 10:30–The present age is an age of homes, fields, and families.
- Luke 18:30–Material rewards are given to us in this life.
- Luke 20:34–The people of this age marry and are given in marriage.
- Romans 12:2–We are not to be conformed to the pattern of this world (age).
- 1 Corinthians 1:20–Philosophy is the wisdom of this age.
- 1 Corinthians 2:6–8–(Man's) wisdom and rulers are of this age.
- 2 Corinthians 4:4–Satan, the god of this age, blinds people's minds to the truth.
- Galatians 1:4–The present age is evil.
- Ephesians 1:20–21–Christ reigns in this present age.
- Ephesians 2:2–The ways of this world (age) are evil.
- 1 Timothy 6:17–Those who are rich in this age are not to hope in their wealth for the next.
- Titus 2:12–We are to live godly lives in this present age.

The Eternal Characterizes the Age to Come

- Matthew 12:32–There is no forgiveness for blasphemy against the Holy Spirit.
- 2 Timothy 4:18–The Lord will bring us to the kingdom of God.
- Mark 10:30; Luke 18:30–Eternal life is a reward.
- Luke 20:35–There will be no marriage or giving in marriage.
- Ephesians 5:5–Immoral people will not inherit the kingdom of God.
- 2 Thessalonians 1:5–Our faith will make us worthy of the kingdom of God.
- 1 Timothy 6:19–The coming age has life that is truly life.
- Ephesians 1:21–Christ will reign in the age to come.
- 1 Corinthians 6:9–10–Evildoers will not inherit the kingdom of God.

---

11   Riddlebarger, *A Case for Amillennialism*, 103–4. Excerpt from *A Case for Amillennialism* by Kim Riddlebarger, copyright © 2013. Used by permission of Baker Books, a division of Baker Publishing Group.

- 1 Corinthians 15:50–Flesh and blood will not inherit the kingdom of God.
- 1 Thessalonians 2:12–We are encouraged to live lives worthy of the kingdom.
- Matthew 13:40–The weeds will be thrown into the fire.
- Galatians 5:21–Those who live evil lives will not inherit the kingdom of God.

We live in the time when the temporary things of this life overlap with the eternal things of our life to come. Paul makes this contrast clear:

> So we do not lose heart. Though our outer self is wasting away, our inner self is being renewed day by day. For this light momentary affliction is preparing for us an eternal weight of glory beyond all comparison, as we look not to the things that are seen but to the things that are unseen. For the things that are seen are transient, but the things that are unseen are eternal. (2 Corinthians 4:16–18)

We live as a part of the current age and as a part of the age to come. The pleasures and struggles of this age are temporary, but the glory to come is eternal.

Already and Not Yet

The comparison and contrast between this age and the age to come is also expressed in terms of the already and the not yet. Through the Spirit, we already live in the age to come, but, because we are still in the fallen body, we do not yet experience the fullness of the new life we have. As Hebrews 6:5 says, we have "tasted the goodness of the word of God and the powers of the age to come," but we still are plagued by sin, suffering, and death. A tension exists between what already is and what will be. However, what we have now in the Spirit is a promise of greater things in the future.

Summary

Recognizing that the last days refer to the time between Christ's first and second comings is vital to properly interpret what the Bible says about the return of Christ. Furthermore, understanding the relationship between "this age" and "the age to come" brings clarity to the study of eschatology. Both restrain us from speculation and arbitrary assignment of "last days" passages to the end. What Christ accomplished in his first coming inaugurated the last days and the age to come. This is often called inaugurated eschatology. What is ours in Christ in the future is ours now by the Holy Spirit (inaugurated eschatology), yet it is not ours in fullness (completed eschatology).

Paul sums up this argument well in his epistle to the church at Ephesus:

> In him you also, when you heard the word of truth, the gospel of your
> salvation, and believed in him, were sealed with the promised Holy Spirit,
> who is the guarantee of our inheritance until we acquire possession of it,
> to the praise of his glory. (Ephesians 1:13–14)

We are still in bodies of fallen flesh, but because we have the Holy Spirit, we are guaranteed the inheritance to come.

Chapter 3

THE KINGDOM OF GOD

A key part of Biblical eschatology is understanding the kingdom of God. As with most eschatological topics, this is one that sparks debate. Is the realization of the kingdom in the future only, or does the kingdom exist now? Is this kingdom an earthly kingdom or a spiritual kingdom? How we understand the kingdom of God has a direct bearing on our understanding of the millennium.

The Kingdom Announced

The New Testament begins with both John the Baptist and Jesus proclaiming a kingdom. For example, in Matthew 3:2, John the Baptist cries out, "Repent, for the kingdom of heaven is at hand." In Mark 1:15 Jesus comes into Galilee teaching "the kingdom of God is at hand." Both messages sound similar, and they are. But a subtle difference in wording exists between Matthew's Gospel and those of Mark, Luke, and John.

In Matthew the kingdom is called the *kingdom of heaven*; in the other gospels, it is called the *kingdom of God*. A careful student of the Word will notice the difference and explore it. Some believe the difference in wording to be significant, signaling two kingdoms: the kingdom of God and the kingdom of heaven. However, by comparing parallel passages from Matthew and Mark, we will conclude the kingdom of God and the kingdom of heaven refer to the same kingdom. Consider Matthew 19:14 and Mark 10:14. Both verses relate Jesus's response when the disciples tried to stop the people from bringing children to him. In Matthew 19:14 Jesus said, "Let the little children come to me and do not hinder them, for to such belongs the kingdom of heaven." Mark 10:14 relates the same story in almost the same words: "Let the children come to me; do not hinder them, for to such belongs the kingdom of God." Matthew ends with "kingdom of heaven," and Mark ends with "kingdom of God." Thus, we must conclude there is one kingdom with two ways to express it.

The King Revealed

For there to be a kingdom there must be a king. In the Old Testament Yahweh is king (Psalm 24:7–10; Isaiah 6:5). In the New Testament Jesus is identified as king. From the start, Matthew calls Jesus the "son of David" (Matthew 1:1). That title is significant because, in 2 Samuel 7:1–17, God made a covenant with King David that he would always have a descendant on the throne of Israel. In the words of God himself: "I will establish the throne of his kingdom forever" (2 Samuel 7:13). Then, in Luke 1:30–33, the angel Gabriel informs Mary that the child she will bear is the fulfillment of God's covenant with David:

> And the angel said to her, "Do not be afraid, Mary, for you have found favor with God. And behold, you will conceive in your womb and bear a son, and you shall call his name Jesus. He will be great and will be called the Son of the Most High. And the Lord God will give to him the throne of his father David, and he will reign over the house of Jacob forever, and of his kingdom there will be no end."

Jesus is that son of David. From the announcement of his birth until his crucifixion, the Gospels present Jesus as king. After his birth, the Magi came asking, "Where is he who has been born king of the Jews?" (Matthew 2:2). At his trial before sending Jesus to the cross, Pilate asked, "Are you the King of the Jews?" (John 18:33). Furthermore, the rest of the New Testament recognizes Jesus as king by calling him *Lord*. Just weeks after Jesus's resurrection, Peter affirmed Jesus as Lord in a sermon he preached on the Day of Pentecost. Look at Acts 2:33–36, where he proclaims that Jesus sits on David's throne:

> Being therefore exalted at the right hand of God, and having received from the Father the promise of the Holy Spirit, he has poured out this that you yourselves are seeing and hearing. For David did not ascend into the heavens, but he himself says,
> "The Lord said to my Lord,
>   'Sit at my right hand,
>   until I make your enemies your footstool.'"
> Let all the house of Israel therefore know for certain that God has made him both Lord and Christ, this Jesus whom you crucified.

God has placed the Lord Jesus on the throne, which makes him "King of kings and Lord of lords" (Revelation 19:16).

The Kingdom Debate

The Bible is clear there is a kingdom, and the New Testament is clear that Jesus is the king. A king must have a realm in which he rules. Jesus sits on the throne, but what is his realm? No end-times theology denies Jesus is the king; however, the timing and location of his kingdom are much in debate.

Dispensationalists perceive the kingdom as future and earthly. They believe the kingdom of heaven and the kingdom of God are two different kingdoms. The kingdom of heaven is God's rule on earth and is tied to the theocratic kingdom of Israel. While Jesus was on earth, he made an offer of a kingdom to Israel, which Israel refused. Therefore, the offer was withdrawn, and the kingdom entered a mystery stage. Riddlebarger gives this explanation:

> Jesus offered this kingdom of heaven to Israel, but when she refused it and rejected him, the offer was withdrawn, and a new redemptive epoch began in which the kingdom is seen as a mystery. The kingdom of God will not come until the millennial age dawns after Christ's second advent. For dispensationalists, then, the kingdom of God is essentially the future earthly reign of Jesus Christ in Jerusalem associated with the glories of an earthly millennial age.[12]

Therefore, in our current age, what dispensationalists call the *church age*, the kingdom is present but in a mysterious form. The true kingdom awaits the earthly millennial reign of Christ when Israel is reconstituted as a theocratic kingdom and Jesus sits on a throne in the earthly Jerusalem.

The classic dispensational view contrasts with the historic reformed view. Those holding the historic reformed view believe the kingdom is present now but will also be consummated in the future. In other words, the kingdom was established with the first coming of Jesus, but the fullness of the kingdom will occur at his second coming. This lines up with what we covered earlier concerning *this age* and the *age to come*. The *age to come* began with the first coming of Jesus and overlaps with *this age*, but the full nature of

---

12   Riddlebarger, *A Case for Amillennialism*, 116. Excerpt from *A Case for Amillennialism*, by Kim Riddlebarger, copyright © 2013. Used by permission of Baker Books, a division of Baker Publishing Group.

the *age to come* will not be realized until Jesus returns. Jesus presents this understanding of the kingdom in Mark 4:26–32:

> And he said, "The kingdom of God is as if a man should scatter seed on the ground. He sleeps and rises night and day, and the seed sprouts and grows; he knows not how. The earth produces by itself, first the blade, then the ear, then the full grain in the ear. But when the grain is ripe, at once he puts in the sickle, because the harvest has come." And he said, "With what can we compare the kingdom of God, or what parable shall we use for it? It is like a grain of mustard seed, which, when sown on the ground, is the smallest of all the seeds on earth, yet when it is sown it grows up and becomes larger than all the garden plants and puts out large branches, so that the birds of the air can make nests in its shade."

Jesus shows the kingdom does not arrive in its fullness in a single cataclysmic event. The kingdom is not established in a moment when Jesus returns, but rather it starts small and grows. Apply what Jesus is saying to the theology of the kingdom of God. Jesus established the kingdom at his first coming. He planted the seed of the kingdom through his death and resurrection, and the kingdom has been growing ever since. Given that the kingdom is not just in the future but also here in the present, we can understand the current realm of the kingdom to be reflected in God's people.[13] However, the kingdom of God in its fullness is much more. Anthony Hoekema (1913–1988) gives this helpful definition of the kingdom of God:

> The kingdom of God ... is to be understood as the reign of God dynamically active in human history through Jesus Christ, the purpose of which is the redemption of God's people from sin and from demonic powers, and the final establishment of the new heavens and the new earth. It means that the great drama of the history of salvation has been inaugurated, and that the new age has been ushered in. The kingdom must not be understood as merely the salvation of certain individuals or even as the reign of God in the hearts of his people; it means nothing less than the reign of God over his entire created universe.[14]

---

13 Riddlebarger, *A Case for Amillennialism*, 119.
14 Anthony A. Hoekema, *The Bible and the Future* (Grand Rapids, MI: Wm. B. Eerdmans Publishing Company, 1979), 45.

Hoekema is emphasizing God's sovereignty. The kingdom of God is God's rule, through Jesus, over everything. Therefore, since it is God's kingdom, he is the one who established it and who rules it. Human effort adds nothing to God's kingdom. As Jesus said in Matthew 16:18, "I will build my church." Furthermore, Hebrews 12:28 makes it clear that we do not assist God in building the kingdom; we receive the kingdom from God:

> Therefore let us be grateful for *receiving* a kingdom that cannot be shaken, and thus let us offer to God acceptable worship, with reverence and awe.

Remember what Daniel 2:44 says:

> And in the days of those kings the God of heaven will set up a kingdom that shall never be destroyed, nor shall the kingdom be left to another people. It shall break in pieces all these kingdoms and bring them to an end, and it shall stand forever.

God sets up a kingdom that will never be destroyed. It will stand forever. God's kingdom is God's sovereignty over his creation and creatures.[15] Sam Storms writes, "The kingdom of God is the redemptive reign of God, or his sovereign lordship, dynamically active to establish his rule among men."[16]

The Present Spiritual Kingdom

Because Jesus is ruling now, his kingdom must be a reality now. But what is the nature of the present kingdom? During the time between the first and second comings of Christ, the kingdom is a spiritual kingdom. In other words, Jesus is ruling through the Holy Spirit. Look at Matthew 12:28:

> But if it is by the Spirit of God that I cast out demons, then the kingdom of God has come upon you.

In a demonstration of power over Satan's realm, Jesus cast out demons by the Holy Spirit. This shows the kingdom of God has come.

---

15   Riddlebarger, *A Case for Amillennialism*, 116.
16   Sam Storms, *Kingdom Come: The Amillennial Alternative* (Fearn, Scotland: Christian Focus Publications, 2013), 339.

Listen in on what Jesus reveals to the Pharisees concerning the kingdom:

> Being asked by the Pharisees when the kingdom of God would come, he answered them, "The kingdom of God is not coming in ways that can be observed, nor will they say, 'Look, here it is!' or 'There!' for behold, the kingdom of God is in the midst of you." (Luke 17:20–21)

Jesus tells the Pharisees that the kingdom of God will not come with a spectacular display. It is already among them in the person of Jesus. When Jesus stood before Pilate, Pilate asked if Jesus was the King of the Jews (John 18:33). In their interaction Jesus couldn't make it any clearer when he said, "My kingdom is not of this world" (John 18:36). (This is the opposite of what many dispensationalists claim.) But if Jesus were interested in setting up an earthly kingdom, Pilate would not have offered to release him. Jesus's kingdom would have been a threat to Rome.

By his own words, Jesus makes it clear that he indeed came into the world to set up a kingdom—but not an earthly kingdom. Jesus established a real kingdom that is currently a spiritual kingdom. He came into the world to bear witness to the truth, and we know that not only does the Holy Spirit testify to the truth, but the Holy Spirit is himself the Spirit of truth (John 16:13). We realize the kingdom today through the Holy Spirit. Paul explains in Romans 14:17 that the kingdom is found in the Holy Spirit:

> For the kingdom of God is not a matter of eating and drinking but of righteousness and peace and joy in the Holy Spirit.

So, Jesus inaugurated the kingdom at his first coming. The present kingdom is redemptive and spiritual and advances by the power of God. Since the kingdom is not fully realized, the advancement of the kingdom means conflict with the forces of evil. Jesus highlighted the conflict in Matthew 10:34:

> Do not think that I have come to bring peace to the earth. I have not come to bring peace, but a sword.

And in 1 Corinthians 15:25, we read that Jesus "must reign until he has put all his enemies under his feet." Jesus has won the victory. He is on the throne. But we must wait for the consummation of his kingdom.

The Future Consummated Kingdom

Even though the kingdom is a present reality in the Holy Spirit, one day the fullness of the kingdom will be realized when we see Jesus face to face. The consummation of the kingdom will occur when Jesus returns. Jesus links the fullness of the kingdom to his return in several parables. He compares the kingdom of heaven to a man who sowed good seed in his field. While the man was sleeping, an enemy came and sowed weeds in the field. Jesus gives this explanation of the parable:

> The one who sows the good seed is the Son of Man. The field is the world, and the good seed is the sons of the kingdom. The weeds are the sons of the evil one, and the enemy who sowed them is the devil. The harvest is the end of the age, and the reapers are angels. Just as the weeds are gathered and burned with fire, so will it be at the end of the age. The Son of Man will send his angels, and they will gather out of his kingdom all causes of sin and all law-breakers, and throw them into the fiery furnace. In that place there will be weeping and gnashing of teeth. Then the righteous will shine like the sun in the kingdom of their Father. He who has ears, let him hear. (Matthew 13:37–43)

When Jesus returns, there will be no more evil. The evildoers will be gathered, judged, and removed from God's kingdom. The righteous will shine in the kingdom, free from all sin. A few verses later, Jesus paints the picture like this:

> Again, the kingdom of heaven is like a net that was thrown into the sea and gathered fish of every kind. When it was full, men drew it ashore and sat down and sorted the good into containers but threw away the bad. So it will be at the end of the age. The angels will come out and separate the evil from the righteous and throw them into the fiery furnace. In that place there will be weeping and gnashing of teeth. (Matthew 13:47–50)

In the parable of the wedding feast (Matthew 22:1–14), only those chosen by God for the kingdom will enter into its fullness. The parable of the ten virgins (Matthew 25:1–13) tells us we must be part of the present kingdom to enjoy the future kingdom.

Paul also speaks of the future kingdom, emphasizing that no unrighteousness will be a part of the kingdom:

> Or do you not know that the unrighteous will not inherit the kingdom of God? Do not be deceived: neither the sexually immoral, nor idolaters, nor adulterers, nor men who practice homosexuality, nor thieves, nor the greedy, nor drunkards, nor revilers, nor swindlers will inherit the kingdom of God. (1 Corinthians 6:9–10)

Galatians 5:21 and Ephesians 5:5 also list those who will not inherit the kingdom of God. And in 1 Corinthians 15, Paul emphasized the consummation of the kingdom with these words:

> For as by a man came death, by a man has come also the resurrection of the dead. For as in Adam all die, so also in Christ shall all be made alive. But each in his own order: Christ the firstfruits, then at his coming those who belong to Christ. Then comes the end, when he delivers the kingdom to God the Father after destroying every rule and every authority and power. For he must reign until he has put all his enemies under his feet. The last enemy to be destroyed is death. For "God has put all things in subjection under his feet." But when it says, "all things are put in subjection," it is plain that he is excepted who put all things in subjection under him. When all things are subjected to him, then the Son himself will also be subjected to him who put all things in subjection under him, that God may be all in all. (1 Corinthians 15:21–26)

In the future kingdom, every enemy—tears, death, mourning, crying, pain—is destroyed. Marvel at what the Lord has in store for his chosen ones when his kingdom is consummated:

> Then I saw a new heaven and a new earth, for the first heaven and the first earth had passed away, and the sea was no more. And I saw the holy city, new Jerusalem, coming down out of heaven from God, prepared as a bride adorned for her husband. And I heard a loud voice from the throne saying, "Behold, the dwelling place of God is with man. He will dwell with them, and they will be his people, and God himself will be with them as their God. He will wipe away every tear from their eyes, and death shall be no more, neither shall there be mourning, nor crying, nor pain anymore, for the former things have passed away." (Revelation 21:1–4)

The future kingdom eliminates all hindrances to joy, and his saints will dwell with God forever.

Summary

The kingdom of God is both now and in the future. This kingdom is God's rule over everything. His son, Jesus, sits on the throne of David as Lord. Jesus initiated his kingdom at his first coming and presently reigns in his people through the Holy Spirit. When Jesus returns, he will banish all evil. Death will be gone and so will pain, grief, tears, and sadness. We will reign with him forever in the fullness of his kingdom. There is no future earthly kingdom with Jesus ruling from Jerusalem. Jesus is ruling now by the Spirit and will rule personally in the new heavens and new earth.

PART 2:

AMILLENNIAL PRESENTATION

Chapters 4–11 present the amillennial understanding of the return of Christ and the events associated with his return.

Chapter 4

THE RETURN OF CHRIST

F
ollowers of Christ look forward to the blessed hope, the return of Christ. Those who belong to Christ may disagree over the details, but we agree on this: the return of Christ is something we long for. Similarly, Christ's glorious return is something to be dreaded by those who do not belong to Christ. Paul explained it to Titus this way:

> For the grace of God has appeared, bringing salvation for all people, training us to renounce ungodliness and worldly passions, and to live self-controlled, upright, and godly lives in the present age, *waiting for our blessed hope, the appearing of the glory of our great God and Savior Jesus Christ*, who gave himself for us to redeem us from all lawlessness and to purify for himself a people for his own possession who are zealous for good works. (Titus 2:11–14)

This passage mentions two appearances: one that has happened and one that will happen. "The grace of God has [already] appeared" refers to when Jesus was born in Bethlehem, lived a perfect life, died on the cross, rose again, and ascended to the Father. In his first appearance, Jesus accomplished salvation for people from "every tribe and language and people and nation" (Revelation 5:9). This salvation brings sanctification as we renounce ungodliness and embrace godliness.

As we live "godly lives in this present age," we wait for the second appearance—"our blessed hope, the appearing of our great God and Savior Jesus Christ." Paul calls the second appearing "our blessed hope." In Romans 8 he gives two characteristics of hope:

> Now hope that is seen is not hope. For who hopes for what he sees?
> But if we hope for what we do not see, we wait for it with patience.
> (Romans 8:24b–25)

Hope is not based on what we see, and hope produces patience. In addition, other characteristics of hope are found in the New Testament. This hope is sure and immovable (Hebrews 6:19). Our hope is a Spirit-empowered hope (Romans 15:13). It is a hope of eternal life (Titus 1:2), and, not surprisingly, it emboldens us (2 Corinthians 3:12).[17]

The New Testament does not present the return of Christ as a point up for theological discussion or debate as to its future reality. Rather, it is biblical truth, vital to our Christian life. Writing to the believers at Thessalonica, Paul identifies some of the events surrounding the return of Christ, telling his readers to "encourage one another with these words" (1 Thessalonians 4:18). Even though the truths about the second coming of Christ are to encourage followers of Christ and give us hope and boldness for our present lives, it's ironic that this glorious doctrine often sparks debate and creates division when it is supposed to build up and embolden. It is not my purpose in this chapter to address the many debatable details concerning Christ's second coming. Instead, I will focus on the signs of the return of Christ, the personal and visible return of Christ, and the disagreement over the number of times Christ returns.

Signs of Christ's Return

Let's briefly look at the signs of Christ's return. Hoekema offers three categories: signs evidencing the grace of God, signs indicating opposition to God, and signs indicating divine judgment.[18]

- Signs evidencing the grace of God:
  - the proclamation of the gospel to all nations
  - the salvation of the fullness of Israel
- Signs indicating opposition to God:
  - tribulation
  - apostasy
  - antichrist

---

17   William Hendriksen, *The Bible on the Life Hereafter* (Grand Rapids, MI: Baker Book House, 1959), 158.

18   Hoekema, *The Bible and the Future*, 137.

- Signs indicating divine judgment:
  - wars
  - earthquakes
  - famines

Proclamation and Salvation

Let's first consider the signs that evidence the grace of God: the proclamation of the gospel to every part of the globe and the full salvation of Israel.

Gospel to All Nations

The proclamation of the gospel began with the Great Commission (Matthew 28:18–20) and continues today, but the gospel must be proclaimed to all nations before Jesus returns. This sign comes from the words of Jesus in Matthew 24:

> And this gospel of the kingdom will be proclaimed throughout the whole world as a testimony to all nations, and then the end will come. (Matthew 24:14)

God intends his gospel to penetrate every part of the world. In Revelation 5:9 and 7:9, John gives us a glimpse that people from every nation, language, and people group will be saved. Revelation 7:9–10 says,

> After this I looked, and behold, a great multitude that no one could number, from every nation, from all tribes and peoples and languages, standing before the throne and before the Lamb, clothed in white robes, with palm branches in their hands, and crying out with a loud voice, "Salvation belongs to our God who sits on the throne, and to the Lamb!"

All nations must hear the gospel and some from each nation must respond before Jesus returns.

All Israel Saved

The second sign that evidences the grace of God is the salvation of the fullness of Israel, which comes from Romans 11:25–27:

> Lest you be wise in your own sight, I do not want you to be unaware of this mystery, brothers: a partial hardening has come upon Israel, until the fullness of the Gentiles has come in. And in this way all Israel will be saved, as it is written,
>
> "The Deliverer will come from Zion,
>
>> he will banish ungodliness from Jacob";
>
> "and this will be my covenant with them
>
>> when I take away their sins."

According to this passage, there is currently a partial hardening of Israel. It is important to note Paul is referring to Israel according to the flesh (ethnic Israelites), not Israel according to the Spirit. This hardening will continue until all the Gentiles that are to be saved are saved.

Paul then makes the statement, "all Israel will be saved." How should we interpret "all Israel will be saved"? Two possibilities demand our consideration.

1. There will be a mass conversion of Jews to Christ just before Jesus returns. Thus, "all Israel" refers to elect Jews saved from every generation plus many Jews saved at the end.[19]
2. The salvation of Jews throughout redemptive history constitutes "all Israel." There will not be a mass conversion of Jews before the return of Christ. Thus, when the last elect physical descendant of Abraham from the last generation has been saved, "all Israel" will be complete.[20]

The belief there will be a large-scale conversion of Jews before the end is not limited to amillennialism. Premillennialists and postmillennialists also believe this (although dispensational premillennialists believe the conversion of Israelites is God resuming his plan for Israel). I hold to the second possibility. Just as God saves Gentiles from every generation, he saves ethnic Israelites from every generation.

Therefore, the phrase "all Israel" equates to the "fullness of the Gentiles." If there is not a mass conversion of Jews just prior to the return of Christ, then "all Israel will be saved" is not technically a sign of Christ's return because Romans 11:25–26 teaches that no elect person—no matter their ethnicity—will remain unsaved before

---

19   See Riddlebarger, *A Case for Amillennialism*, 207–21for a defense of this position.
20   See Hoekema, *The Bible and the Future*, 139–47 for a defense of this position.

the second coming of Christ. This is a fulfillment of the first sign, the gospel will go to all nations.

However, the manner of the salvation of ethnic Israelites is not an issue to divide over. God determined the number of the elect, both Jew and Gentile, before the foundation of the world and he will save them all without losing a single one. Scripture makes this clear: when the "fullness of the Gentiles has come in," we can be sure "all Israel" will have been saved, and then Christ will return.

Tribulation, Apostasy, and Antichrist

Another reality signals the pending return of Christ: opposition to the Lord. The three signs of opposition to God—tribulation, apostasy, and antichrist—work in concert.[21] It comes as no surprise that all three are active in our era.

Jesus spoke of the certainty of tribulation, saying,

> I have said these things to you, that in me you may have peace. In the world you will have tribulation. But take heart; I have overcome the world. (John 16:33)

Both Jesus and the apostles made it clear that aligning with Jesus would bring tribulation throughout the gospel age (John 15:20; Acts 14:22; Romans 8:17; 2 Timothy 3:12; Revelation 1:9).

Apostasy, the second kind of opposition, involves those who appear to be godly but are not truly regenerate. This kind of opposition is not limited to the time just before the return of Christ (Hebrews 3:12–14; 6:4–6; 2 Peter 2:20–22; 1 Timothy 4:1; 2 Timothy 3:1–5; 1 John 2:19). The New Testament writers make it clear that people will abandon Christianity until Christ returns.

Concerning antichrist, 1 John 2:18 tells us antichrist is a present reality, not just one reserved for the future:

> Children, it is the last hour, and as you have heard that antichrist is coming, so now many antichrists have come. Therefore we know that it is the last hour.

---

21   See chapter 5, "Satan's Little Season."

We know we are in the last hour because there are false christs.[22] Therefore, tribulation, apostasy, and antichrist are present realities, but there will be an intensification of each before the second coming of Christ.[23]

Wars, Earthquakes, and Famines

The signs that indicate divine judgment—wars, earthquakes, and famines—are spread throughout human history. The Bible does not build a case for an increase in wars, earthquakes, and famines in proximity to Christ's return. Additionally, the ongoing signs evidencing the grace of God and those indicating opposition to God will reach their fullness before Christ returns. For this reason, I addressed only the signs evidencing the grace of God (gospel to all nations and the fullness of Israel) and the signs indicating opposition to God (tribulation, apostasy, and antichrist).

It is worth noting that none of these signs can be used to pinpoint when Christ will appear again. God provides these signs to encourage us to persevere in the spread of the gospel. We must remain faithful while enduring the opposition we will encounter.

Personal and Visible Return

Let there be no mistake: Jesus is coming again. Even though believers differ in the details, we all look forward to the personal and visible return of Christ. At the ascension of Jesus, the apostles were gazing up into heaven. Two men in white robes appeared next to them and asked a question, then they taught an important truth:

> Men of Galilee, why do you stand looking into heaven? This Jesus, who was taken up from you into heaven, will come in the same way as you saw him go into heaven. (Acts 1:11)

---

22 Also, see Matthew 24:5, 23–24; 1 John 2:22; 4:1–3. Furthermore, John's use of "last hour" refers to the New Testament age. John sometimes uses "hour" to refer to a point in time (see John 7:30; 12:23; 13:1), and he sometimes uses "hour" to refer to an extended period of time. The latter applies to 1 John 2:18. For example, in John 4:23, Jesus tells the woman at the well, "But the hour is coming, and is now here, when the true worshipers will worship the Father in spirit and truth, for the Father is seeking such people to worship him." Jesus did not mean that his time with the Samaritan woman was the only time to worship in spirit and truth. We are still in that time. See chapter 8, "The General Resurrection," for a discussion of the use of "hour" in John 5:25–29.

23 See chapter 5, "Satan's Little Season."

Note these men, angels actually, tell the apostles "this Jesus" that they see ascending will be the one returning. "This Jesus" is the Word that became flesh (John 1:14), the one who was born of Mary and placed in a manger. Jesus is forever the God-man, and he is the one who will return.

Second, Christ's return will be visible. The angels told the gazing apostles Jesus "will come in the same way as you *saw* him go into heaven." John clearly states just how evident the appearing of Jesus will be:

> Behold, he is coming with the clouds, and every eye will see him, even those who pierced him, and all tribes of the earth will wail on account of him. Even so. Amen. (Revelation 1:7)

Jesus will descend with the clouds the same way he ascended (Acts 1:9), and "every eye will see him." The widespread agreement on the personal and visible return of Jesus is a rallying point across Christianity.

One Return

While believers agree Jesus will return, they disagree concerning the number of times he returns. Some say Jesus will return once, while others say twice, and still others say three times.

The popular dispensational view is Jesus will return first *for* his saints and then *with* his saints. They call the first return of Jesus the "rapture," which is secret because it will not be visible to everyone. The term itself comes from the idea of being caught up or carried away. They believe the rapture, which can happen at any moment, is when Jesus will appear in the air to gather his saints. The bodies of dead believers will be resurrected and believers who are alive at that time will ascend to be with Jesus.

The dispensational timeline continues after the rapture with seven years of severe tribulation on the earth. This "Great Tribulation" will include the revealing of the man of lawlessness and a great apostasy across humanity. At the end of the tribulation, Jesus will return along with the church—this time to establish his millennial kingdom on the earth with his throne in Jerusalem. This return of Christ was announced to the disciples in Acts 1:11.

So, according to dispensationalism, the return of Christ is twofold: a secret rapture, seen only by believers, followed by the final return of Christ, seen by all people.

There is another view of Christ's return that I believe is on strong scriptural footing. It holds that Christ returns only once. Let's explore that view next by looking at what Jesus and Paul say about the second coming.

Jesus

First, let's consider the words Jesus spoke concerning his return. Matthew records these words:

> For as the lightning comes from the east and shines as far as the west, so will be the coming of the Son of Man. (Matthew 24:27)

In verse 26 Jesus says you won't need to go looking for him because his return will be like lightning in the sky, visible to everyone (v. 27).

When Jesus returns, he will sit on his throne and judge all people:

> When the Son of Man comes in his glory, and all the angels with him, then he will sit on his glorious throne. Before him will be gathered all the nations, and he will separate people one from another as a shepherd separates the sheep from the goats. (Matthew 25:31–32)

Therefore, judgment occurs at the point when Jesus returns. Not only does this eliminate a two-fold return, but it also eliminates the earthly millennium occurring after Christ's return. Luke records Jesus telling a parable emphasizing the need to be ready for his return. The parable ends like this:

> But know this, that if the master of the house had known at what hour the thief was coming, he would not have left his house to be broken into. You also must be ready, for the Son of Man is coming at an hour you do not expect. (Luke 12:39–40)

If all we had to go on was what Jesus said in Luke 12:39–40, you could agree with the idea of a secret rapture. Jesus will come at any moment—and we need to be ready. But Scripture interprets Scripture, and Peter asks a clarifying question in verse 41: "Lord, are you telling this parable for us or for all?" Jesus doesn't directly answer Peter's question, but his response indicates the parable is not just for those who are in Christ. It is meant for all. The faithful and wise manager will be rewarded (vs. 42–43), but the unfaithful servant will be judged (vs. 44–48). Again, we see a separation of the righteous and the unrighteous at the point when Jesus returns.

Luke relates another parable of God's justice in the story of the persistent widow in Luke 18:1–8. A widow continues to go to the unjust judge to seek justice against her adversary. The unjust judge eventually grants the widow's request because she wears him down. The argument of the parable is from the lesser to the greater. If the unjust judge will eventually give justice, how much more will God give justice to those who continually appear in his presence through prayer? Notice what Jesus said in verse 8:

> I tell you, [God] will give justice to them speedily. Nevertheless, when the Son of Man comes, will he find faith on earth? (Luke 18:8)

God's elect will get justice against the unrighteous. That is an encouragement to God's people, but Jesus ends with the question, "When the Son of Man comes, will he find faith on the earth?" Given the context of injustice against the widow and the need to persevere in prayer, the implication is clear: there will be much injustice against God's people by the time Jesus returns. Thus, Jesus connects justice with his return.

Jesus cannot be referring to the dispensational secret rapture since there is no judgment for the unbeliever at that time. Also, there is no secret rapture that rescues the church from tribulation. Jesus's question implies tribulation for his people, not escape from tribulation. When Jesus returns, he executes judgment against the wicked because of the persecution they brought against his church.[24]

Paul

The apostle Paul also weighs in on Jesus's return in judgment. In 2 Thessalonians 2:5–10, Paul writes about the "lawless one," whom "the Lord Jesus will kill with the breath of his mouth and bring to nothing by the appearance of his coming" (v. 8). This passage follows Paul's boasting concerning the Thessalonians' faithfulness under persecution:

> Therefore we ourselves boast about you in the churches of God for your steadfastness and faith in all your persecutions and in the afflictions that you are enduring. (2 Thessalonians 1:4)

Paul continues his explanation concerning the return of Christ. When Jesus returns, he pours out his vengeance on "those who do not know God and on those who do not obey the gospel of our Lord Jesus." His argument goes like this:

> This is evidence of the righteous judgment of God, that you may be considered worthy of the kingdom of God, for which you are also suffering—

---

24   See chapter 9, "The Final Judgment."

since indeed God considers it just to repay with affliction those who afflict you, and to grant relief to you who are afflicted as well as to us, when the Lord Jesus is revealed from heaven with his mighty angels in flaming fire, inflicting vengeance on those who do not know God and on those who do not obey the gospel of our Lord Jesus. They will suffer the punishment of eternal destruction, away from the presence of the Lord and from the glory of his might, when he comes on that day to be glorified in his saints, and to be marveled at among all who have believed, because our testimony to you was believed. (2 Thessalonians 1:5–10)

God will eternally afflict those who tormented his people.

Paul also expands on Jesus's reference to the time of his return being unknown. Jesus refers to "the thief" in Matthew 24:43. Just as we do not know when a thief might break in, we do not know the time of Christ's return. In 1 Thessalonians 5:1–11, Paul said Jesus "will come like a thief in the night." Take a look at that thought in context:

Now concerning the times and the seasons, brothers, you have no need to have anything written to you. For you yourselves are fully aware that the day of the Lord will come like a thief in the night. While people are saying, "There is peace and security," then sudden destruction will come upon them as labor pains come upon a pregnant woman, and they will not escape. But you are not in darkness, brothers, for that day to surprise you like a thief. For you are all children of light, children of the day. We are not of the night or of the darkness. So then let us not sleep, as others do, but let us keep awake and be sober. For those who sleep, sleep at night, and those who get drunk, are drunk at night. But since we belong to the day, let us be sober, having put on the breastplate of faith and love, and for a helmet the hope of salvation. For God has not destined us for wrath, but to obtain salvation through our Lord Jesus Christ, who died for us so that whether we are awake or asleep we might live with him. Therefore encourage one another and build one another up, just as you are doing. (1 Thessalonians 5:1–11)

Paul brings several truths into focus in this passage. While the timing of the day of the Lord is as unknown as the arrival of "a thief in the night" (v. 2), it should not be feared by those who are Christ's. The unbelieving world is not looking for Christ to return, so his return will be an unpleasant surprise. However, we who know Christ are ever looking for his return. We should not fear the day of the Lord because "God has not destined us for wrath" (v. 9). God's wrath will be poured out when Jesus returns. Paul ends with an admonishment to encourage one another with this truth.

Dispensationalism will sometimes point to 1 Thessalonians 5:9 to advance the idea of believers being taken by a secret rapture before the time of tribulation:

> For God has not destined us for wrath, but to obtain salvation through our
> Lord Jesus Christ.

They believe the church cannot be present during a time of great tribulation because God's people will never be under his wrath. I agree. God's people are not destined for God's wrath, but tribulation itself is not wrath.

While believers are immune from the wrath of God, we are not immune from the wrath of man. In fact, God's people are destined for tribulation. Jesus said, "I have said these things to you, that in me you may have peace. In the world you will have tribulation. But take heart; I have overcome the world" (John 16:33). The teaching of the New Testament is that the people of God will experience great tribulation.[25] This reality eliminates the need for a twofold return of Christ: a secret rapture followed seven years later by the visible return of Christ.

The primary passage used to teach a secret rapture comes from Paul in 1 Thessalonians 4:

> But we do not want you to be uninformed, brothers, about those who
> are asleep, that you may not grieve as others do who have no hope. For
> since we believe that Jesus died and rose again, even so, through Jesus,
> God will bring with him those who have fallen asleep. For this we declare
> to you by a word from the Lord, that we who are alive, who are left until
> the coming of the Lord, will not precede those who have fallen asleep. For
> the Lord himself will descend from heaven with a cry of command, with
> the voice of an archangel, and with the sound of the trumpet of God. And
> the dead in Christ will rise first. Then we who are alive, who are left, will
> be caught up together with them in the clouds to meet the Lord in the air,
> and so we will always be with the Lord. Therefore encourage one another
> with these words. (1 Thessalonians 4:13–18)

---

25 See chapter 5, "Satan's Little Season."

Unbelievers are not mentioned in this passage. The focus is on believers being with Christ. The dead in Christ are raised first then those who are alive that belong to Christ are "caught up together" with the raised believers. All meet Jesus in the air.

Clearly, Jesus is coming *for* his saints (v. 15 refers to "the coming of the Lord"). The end of verse 17 says, "And so we will always be with the Lord." The dispensational assumption is this refers to believers being removed from the earth and being with the Lord during the seven-year tribulation that is occurring on the earth. But there is no reason to assume this since the Greek word translated *coming* (*parousia*) in verse 15 is also used for Jesus coming *with* his saints.

In 1 Thessalonians 3:13 Paul prays "that he (the Lord) may establish your hearts blameless in holiness before our God and Father, at the *coming* of our Lord Jesus *with* all his saints." This implies Jesus coming for his saints and with his saints is the same event. Jesus comes with his saints who have already died, so they are reunited with their resurrected bodies, and he comes for the saints alive at the time of his return.[26] All the saints then descend with Jesus to the new earth.

Paul concludes with a command to "encourage one another with these words"— words that reveal all who are in Christ will forever be in his presence. Paul's purpose in this passage was to give hope. He did not want the Thessalonians to "grieve as others do who have no hope." Those who are "asleep" will not miss the return of Christ. The return of Christ is the great hope for all believers, living or dead.

The same word (*coming*) is used when Jesus comes to destroy the man of lawlessness:

> And then the lawless one will be revealed, whom the Lord Jesus will kill with the breath of his mouth and bring to nothing by the appearance of his coming. (2 Thessalonians 2:8)

This is a clear reference to the second coming of Christ, not a secret rapture. Therefore, we must conclude that the biblical support for a secret rapture is lacking. But the Bible makes it plain: Jesus will visibly return once to powerfully wrap up the current age and begin the final state.

Summary

Just as certain as the first coming of Christ was, so also is the second coming of Christ. The gospel will be proclaimed throughout the earth, and all the elect, both Jew and Gentile,

---

26　Hoekema, *The Bible and the Future*, 169.

will be saved before Christ returns. Until he returns, Christians will experience tribulation, some who falsely claimed to be Christians will apostatize, and false christs will abound. After intense tribulation, apostasy, and antichrist, Jesus will return only once as the Son of Man in power and glory. Until that time, we are to proclaim the Word faithfully with a sure and certain hope that God is faithful and that Jesus will return to usher in the final state.

Chapter 5

SATAN'S LITTLE SEASON

In the previous chapter, I introduced the signs of opposition to God: tribulation, apostasy, and antichrist. Furthermore, I explained how all the signs of opposition to God work together. In this chapter, I want to investigate the intensification of tribulation, apostasy, and antichrist proximate to the return of Christ.

To recap, throughout the time between the first and second comings of Christ, the Bible promises tribulation, apostasy, and antichrists. Jesus said in John 16:33,

> I have said these things to you, that in me you may have peace. In the world you will have tribulation. But take heart; I have overcome the world.

Peter warns us of apostasy during our time:

> But false prophets also arose among the people, just as there will be false teachers among you, who will secretly bring in destructive heresies, even denying the Master who bought them, bringing upon themselves swift destruction. And many will follow their sensuality, and because of them the way of truth will be blasphemed. (2 Peter 2:1–2)

Concerning antichrists in our day, we read in 1 John 2:18,

> Children, it is the last hour, and as you have heard that antichrist is
> coming, so now many antichrists have come. Therefore we know that it
> is the last hour.

Too many Christians (especially those in the West who have faced minimal opposition to Christianity) have limited these warnings to the time just before the return of
Christ, but the Scripture does not allow that. The Bible does indicate a time of severe
tribulation, great apostasy, and a final antichrist at the time of Christ's return. Based on
Revelation 20:1–3, some have called this time of intensification "Satan's little season":

> Then I saw an angel coming down from heaven, holding in his hand the
> key to the bottomless pit and a great chain. And he seized the dragon,
> that ancient serpent, who is the devil and Satan, and bound him for a
> thousand years, and threw him into the pit, and shut it and sealed it over
> him, so that he might not deceive the nations any longer, until the thou-
> sand years were ended. After that he must be released for a little while.

Notice at the end of verse 3 that Satan "must be released for a little while." The KJV
says, "He [Satan] must be loosed *a little season*." Thus, "Satan's little season" is a common
designation for the period of Satan's release from the bottomless pit. The dispensationalist's definition of Satan's little season and what I present in this chapter are very different,
due to the differences in our interpretive approach to Revelation.

Interpreting Revelation

In chapter 1 we considered the genre and audience of Revelation. It is apocalyptic literature, full of signs and symbols, written to people undergoing persecution. But what else
do we need to keep in mind concerning how we read Revelation?

First, let's remember the purpose of Revelation is to comfort the church in its
struggle against the forces of evil by showing that God rules over all things. The theme
of Revelation is Christ and his church are victorious over the dragon (Satan) and his
helpers. The apostle John wrote during the reign of Domitian (AD 81–96) to the seven
churches in Asia Minor, but what John wrote to the seven churches is relevant for
believers of all times.[27]

---

27 William Hendriksen, *More Than Conquerors* (Grand Rapids, MI: Baker Books, 1940, 1967,
    1998), 7–11.

Second, we need to understand the structure of Revelation. The book consists of seven visions. Each vision spans the period from the first coming of Christ to the second, but each vision has a different emphasis. The seven visions are:

- Christ in the midst of the seven golden lampstands, the church on earth (chapters 1–3)
- The book with the seven seals (chapters 4–7)
- The seven trumpets of judgment (chapters 8–11)
- The woman and the male child persecuted by the dragon and his helpers, or aspects of warfare and salvation (chapters 12–14)
- The seven bowls of wrath (chapters 15–16)
- The fall of the great prostitute and the beasts, or victory for Christ (chapters 17–19)
- The final judgment followed by the new heavens and new earth (chapters 20–22)

The seven visions can be grouped into two major divisions. The first major division (chapters 1–11) consists of the first three visions, and the second major division (chapters 12–22) consists of the remaining four visions.

- The first division reveals the church indwelt by Christ and persecuted by the world. The church is avenged, protected, and victorious.
- The second division reveals the deeper spiritual background of the struggle between the church and the world. It is essentially a war between Christ and the dragon in which Christ and his church are victorious.[28]

Understanding the genre, audience, purpose, and structure of Revelation will help guide our approach to this glorious book.

The Binding of Satan

Let's turn now to the binding of Satan in Revelation 20:1–3:

> Then I saw an angel coming down from heaven, holding in his hand the key to the bottomless pit and a great chain. And he seized the dragon,

---

28 Hendriksen, *More Than Conquerors*, 21–23. Other Bible commentators present more nuanced structures for Revelation, but what Hendriksen presents is a good starting point.

that ancient serpent, who is the devil and Satan, and bound him for a thousand years, and threw him into the pit, and shut it and sealed it over him, so that he might not deceive the nations any longer, until the thousand years were ended. After that he must be released for a little while.

Since the seven visions of Revelation generally start with the first coming of Christ and end with the second, the visions run parallel. Chapter 20 is the beginning of a new vision, taking us back to the first coming of Christ. Therefore, the one thousand years represent the time between the two comings of Christ. During this time Satan is bound. This is one of the primary places where the amillennial view is scorned. How can we say Satan is bound now? Doesn't Peter say Satan is currently prowling "around like a roaring lion seeking someone to devour" (1 Peter 5:8)? Doesn't Paul say in 2 Corinthians 4:4 that "the god of this world," meaning Satan, "has blinded the minds of unbelievers"? As premillennial opponents of amillennialism often say, "If Satan is bound, he is on a really long leash." I understand these objections, but they are based on an understanding of binding that isn't derived by comparing Scripture with Scripture. Let's examine the case amillennialists build to claim Satan is presently bound.

First, consider how Jesus refers to binding. Matthew tells the story of Jesus casting out a demon from a blind and mute man. Because of this, the people wonder if Jesus could be the promised son of David. The Pharisees, however, claim Jesus cast out the demon by the power of Satan. Take a look at Jesus's response in Matthew 12:25–29:

> Knowing their thoughts, he said to them, "Every kingdom divided against itself is laid waste, and no city or house divided against itself will stand. And if Satan casts out Satan, he is divided against himself. How then will his kingdom stand? And if I cast out demons by Beelzebul, by whom do your sons cast them out? Therefore they will be your judges. But if it is by the Spirit of God that I cast out demons, then the kingdom of God has come upon you. Or how can someone enter a strong man's house and plunder his goods, unless he first binds the strong man? Then indeed he may plunder his house."

Jesus says he casts out demons by the power of the Holy Spirit, which indicates the kingdom of God has come.[29] Associated with the coming of the kingdom is the binding

---

29   See chapter 3, "The Kingdom of God."

of the "strong man," which represents Satan. The word used here for *binds* comes from the same Greek word used in Revelation 20 for the binding of Satan. Jesus claims he must bind Satan in order to plunder Satan's realm.

Second, in Revelation 20:1–3, Satan's binding limits him only in one area: "He cannot deceive the nations." In other words, Satan cannot stop the spread of the gospel to the whole world. Matthew 28:18–20 supports this:

> And Jesus came and said to them, "All authority in heaven and on earth has been given to me. Go therefore and make disciples of all nations, baptizing them in the name of the Father and of the Son and of the Holy Spirit, teaching them to observe all that I have commanded you. And behold, I am with you always, to the end of the age."

Because Jesus has *all authority* in heaven and on earth (that is, in the heavenly and earthly realms), we are to go to *all nations* and make disciples. Also, Jesus said in Matthew 16:18, "I will build my church, and the gates of hell shall not prevail against it." Gates are defensive structures, but even the gates of hell cannot withstand the power of the gospel. Furthermore, we read in Hebrews 2:14–15,

> Since therefore the children share in flesh and blood, he himself likewise partook of the same things, that through death he might destroy the one who has the power of death, that is, the devil, and deliver all those who through fear of death were subject to lifelong slavery.

Through his death, Jesus "destroys" or utterly defeats the devil in order to free the enslaved.[30] Death cannot maintain its hold on humanity when the one with the power of death has been defeated. This means the devil cannot restrain Jesus from his mission to build his Church. Jesus is the one who binds Satan and expands the kingdom of God. Jesus has all authority and is building his Church by plundering the world, which "lies in the power of the evil one" (1 John 5:19). We see the ultimate result of Satan being bound in Revelation 7:9–10:

---

30   Other translations of this verse also emphasize that Satan is powerless to stop the Gospel. The LSB says Jesus "Himself likewise also partook of the same, that through death He might render powerless him who had the power of death," and the NIV says Jesus "shared in their humanity so that by his death he might break the power of him who holds the power of death."

> After this I looked, and behold, a great multitude that no one could number, from every nation, from all tribes and peoples and languages, standing before the throne and before the Lamb, clothed in white robes, with palm branches in their hands, and crying out with a loud voice, "Salvation belongs to our God who sits on the throne, and to the Lamb!"

People from every part of the globe will rejoice before the Lamb. Satan can deceive individuals, but Satan cannot stop God's plan for salvation throughout the earth. This is what amillennialists mean when we say Satan is bound.

Satan Is Released

Although Satan currently is bound, at the end of the one thousand years Satan will be released for a little while. This will occur just before the return of Christ. Whereas during the time between the cross and the second coming Satan could not stop the spread of the gospel or the expansion of the Church, at the time just prior to the return of Christ, God will remove that restriction. Look at Revelation 20:7–10:

> And when the thousand years are ended, Satan will be released from his prison and will come out to deceive the nations that are at the four corners of the earth, Gog and Magog, to gather them for battle; their number is like the sand of the sea. And they marched up over the broad plain of the earth and surrounded the camp of the saints and the beloved city, but fire came down from heaven and consumed them, and the devil who had deceived them was thrown into the lake of fire and sulfur where the beast and the false prophet were, and they will be tormented day and night forever and ever.

After he is released, Satan will deceive the nations. He will gather them for battle against the people of God. Note the parallels to this in other parts of Revelation.

Revelation 11

In Revelation 11 we find the two witnesses. These two witnesses are a picture of the Church, but especially the public witness of the Church. Verses 1–3 introduce the two witnesses:

> Then I was given a measuring rod like a staff, and I was told, "Rise and measure the temple of God and the altar and those who worship there,

but do not measure the court outside the temple; leave that out, for it is given over to the nations, and they will trample the holy city for forty-two months. And I will grant authority to my two witnesses, and they will prophesy for 1,260 days, clothed in sackcloth."

The temple refers to the Church (1 Corinthians 3:16; Ephesians 2:21). The 1,260 days, which is forty-two months, refers to the time between the first and second comings of Christ. During this time, there are two witnesses. These are not reappearances of Elijah and Moses but rather represent the power of the public witness of the Church. The requirement of two witnesses to provide testimony of guilt is given both in Deuteronomy 17:6 and Matthew 18:16:

On the evidence of two witnesses or of three witnesses the one who is to die shall be put to death; a person shall not be put to death on the evidence of one witness. (Deuteronomy 17:6)

But if he does not listen, take one or two others along with you, that every charge may be established by the evidence of two or three witnesses. (Matthew 18:16)

Thus, the "two witnesses" in Revelation 11 represent the powerful witness of Christ's church in the world. Notice what happens in Revelation 11:7–12:

And when they have finished their testimony, the beast that rises from the bottomless pit will make war on them and conquer them and kill them, and their dead bodies will lie in the street of the great city that symbolically is called Sodom and Egypt, where their Lord was crucified. For three and a half days some from the peoples and tribes and languages and nations will gaze at their dead bodies and refuse to let them be placed in a tomb, and those who dwell on the earth will rejoice over them and make merry and exchange presents, because these two prophets had been a torment to those who dwell on the earth. But after the three and a half days a breath of life from God entered them, and they stood up on their feet, and great fear fell on those who saw them. Then they heard a loud voice from heaven saying to them, "Come up here!" And they went up to heaven in a cloud, and their enemies watched them.

Just as in chapter 20, an enemy, this time the beast, is released from the bottomless pit. When Satan was released, he went out to make war against the saints; so also, this beast makes war on the two witnesses. The witnesses are silenced for a short period before Jesus returns and takes his people home. Just as John said there are already antichrists (1 John 2:18), the public witness of the church is already silenced in various places. China has many believers, but the Chinese church has little public witness due to governmental oppression (which, as we will see, is represented by the beast in Revelation 13). Notice that their dead bodies lie in the street of the city represented by "Sodom, Egypt, and the city where their Lord was crucified" (v. 8), which is Jerusalem. Sodom represents immorality, Egypt represents oppressive governments, and Jerusalem represents false or works-based religion. Therefore, we see that immorality, persecuting governments, and false religion are what silence the public witness of the Church. This is true today, and it will be true worldwide during Satan's little season.

Revelation 12–14

This same pattern is found in Revelation 12–14. This vision again starts with the first coming of Christ, but this time there is a dragon, which is identified as Satan, who wants to devour the child that is born of the woman. This woman represents Israel, who brought forth the Messiah. Revelation 12:7–14 describes the dragon's opposition to the woman:

> Now war arose in heaven, Michael and his angels fighting against the dragon. And the dragon and his angels fought back, but he was defeated, and there was no longer any place for them in heaven. And the great dragon was thrown down, that ancient serpent, who is called the devil and Satan, the deceiver of the whole world—he was thrown down to the earth, and his angels were thrown down with him. And I heard a loud voice in heaven, saying, "Now the salvation and the power and the king-dom of our God and the authority of his Christ have come, for the accuser of our brothers has been thrown down, who accuses them day and night before our God. And they have conquered him by the blood of the Lamb and by the word of their testimony, for they loved not their lives even unto death. Therefore, rejoice, O heavens and you who dwell in them! But woe to you, O earth and sea, for the devil has come down to you in great wrath, because he knows that his time is short!" And when the dragon saw that he had been thrown down to the earth, he pursued the woman who had given birth to the male child. But the woman was given the two

wings of the great eagle so that she might fly from the serpent into the wilderness, to the place where she is to be nourished for a time, and times, and half a time.

We have the picture of the victory of Christ on the cross, followed by the dragon's pursuit of the woman, who now represents the Church. However, the woman is given the wings of an eagle so that she might fly to a place where she is protected for "a time, times, and half a time," which is forty-two months, the time between the first and second comings of Christ. Isaiah 40:28–31 gives us the understanding of the "wings of an eagle" reference:

> Have you not known? Have you not heard?
> The LORD is the everlasting God,
>   the Creator of the ends of the earth.
> He does not faint or grow weary;
>   his understanding is unsearchable.
> He gives power to the faint,
>   and to him who has no might he increases strength.
> Even youths shall faint and be weary,
>   and young men shall fall exhausted;
> but they who wait for the LORD shall renew their strength;
>   they shall mount up with wings like eagles;
> they shall run and not be weary;
>   they shall walk and not faint.

The Lord sustains his people through suffering and trial. Waiting patiently on the Lord is compared to soaring like an eagle. There is a similar picture in Exodus 19:3–4:

> The LORD called to him out of the mountain, saying, "Thus you shall say to the house of Jacob, and tell the people of Israel: 'You yourselves have seen what I did to the Egyptians, and how I bore you on eagles' wings and brought you to myself.'"

God uses the imagery of eagles' wings to describe the deliverance of Israel from Egypt. Therefore, the picture in Revelation 12 shows us that during the present age, God sustains and protects his Church. However, in Revelation 13, we are introduced to the beast, which represents world governments. Notice the activity of the beast:

> And the beast was given a mouth uttering haughty and blasphemous words, and it was allowed to exercise authority for forty-two months. It opened its mouth to utter blasphemies against God, blaspheming his name and his dwelling, that is, those who dwell in heaven. Also it was allowed to make war on the saints and to conquer them. And authority was given it over every tribe and people and language and nation, and all who dwell on earth will worship it, everyone whose name has not been written before the foundation of the world in the book of life of the Lamb who was slain. (Revelation 13:5–8)

Again, we see that forty-two-month period which represents the period between the first and second advent of Christ. However, God allows the beast to make war on the saints. This happens throughout the present age. However, the beast not only makes war on the saints, it also eventually conquers them. There is a time of severe persecution for the Church. The rest of this vision spans the latter half of chapter 13, which introduces us to the false prophet and leads to Christ's return in judgment in chapter 14.

2 Thessalonians 2

In his second letter to the Thessalonians, Paul discusses the man of lawlessness and the mystery of lawlessness in the context of the second coming of Christ:

> Now concerning the coming of our Lord Jesus Christ and our being gathered together to him, we ask you, brothers, not to be quickly shaken in mind or alarmed, either by a spirit or a spoken word, or a letter seeming to be from us, to the effect that the day of the Lord has come. Let no one deceive you in any way. For that day will not come, unless the rebellion comes first, and the man of lawlessness is revealed, the son of destruction, who opposes and exalts himself against every so-called god or object of worship, so that he takes his seat in the temple of God, proclaiming himself to be God. Do you not remember that when I was still with you I told you these things? And you know what is restraining him now so that he may be revealed in his time. For the mystery of lawlessness is already at work. Only he who now restrains it will do so until he is out of the way. And then the lawless one will be revealed, whom the Lord Jesus will kill with the breath of his mouth and bring to nothing by the appearance of his coming. The coming of the lawless one is by the

activity of Satan with all power and false signs and wonders, and with all wicked deception for those who are perishing, because they refused to love the truth and so be saved. Therefore God sends them a strong delusion, so that they may believe what is false, in order that all may be condemned who did not believe the truth but had pleasure in unrighteousness. (2 Thessalonians 2:1–12)

This rebellion or apostasy must happen before the return of Christ—and so must the revealing of the man of lawlessness. There are several things we learn about this man of lawlessness:

- The man of lawlessness will come from the rebellion (v. 3).
- The man of lawlessness will be an actual person, not simply some type of spirit of the age manifested in society in general (note the use of *he*, *him*, and *his*).
- The man of lawlessness will be worshiped, which means he is a threat to the Church.
- The man of lawlessness will use deceptive miracles and false teaching (vs. 9–10).
- The man of lawlessness is revealed after what is restraining him is removed. There is much speculation as to what (v. 6) or who (v. 7) is restraining. I submit we do not know the identity of the restrainer, other than we know God is ultimately in control of all that happens. The restraining of the Antichrist is tied to the binding of Satan. In God's providence, the ultimate manifestation of the Antichrist is being withheld until the time God has ordained for him to be revealed, which is when Satan is released at the end of the one thousand years.
- The man of lawlessness will be destroyed at the coming of Christ (v. 8).[31]

It is no surprise that, over the centuries, many people have been signaled out as the Antichrist, such as Emperor Nero, various popes, Hitler, or Stalin. So, the sign of antichrist, just like the signs of tribulation and apostasy, has been evident throughout the gospel age, but there is a final antichrist coming.[32] When the man of lawlessness is released, there will be a rebellion against the Church, and Satan will actively lead the rebellion through the man of lawlessness. All this will occur when Satan is released from the bottomless pit.

---

31 Hoekema, *The Bible and the Future*, 159–61.
32 Hoekema, *The Bible and the Future*, 162.

Matthew 24

In chapter 12 I will look at Jesus's teaching at the Mount of Olives (called the Olivet Discourse) from an amillennial perspective. There Jesus predicted the abomination of desolation. This was partially fulfilled in the destruction of Jerusalem by the Roman general Titus in AD 70. However, it points to a greater fulfillment before Jesus comes. In Matthew 24:29 Jesus refers to the "tribulation of those days." This is referring to the final tribulation because, after that tribulation, Jesus returns (Matthew 24:30).

Revelation 16

During the period between the first and second comings of Christ, the Church grows because Satan is bound. As represented by the two witnesses, the Church proclaims the gospel. But even though Satan is bound, he can persecute the Church. However, the Church is protected in that Jesus gives his people the faith and power to endure. There is coming a day, though, when the restraints on Satan will be removed, and he will pour out his fury. He will make war on the saints and many who appear to be saints will fall away. This is seen in multiple places, but it is also found in the sixth bowl of wrath in Revelation 16:12–16:

> The sixth angel poured out his bowl on the great river Euphrates, and its water was dried up, to prepare the way for the kings from the east. And I saw, coming out of the mouth of the dragon and out of the mouth of the beast and out of the mouth of the false prophet, three unclean spirits like frogs. For they are demonic spirits, performing signs, who go abroad to the kings of the whole world, to assemble them for battle on the great day of God the Almighty. ("Behold, I am coming like a thief! Blessed is the one who stays awake, keeping his garments on, that he may not go about naked and be seen exposed!") And they assembled them at the place that in Hebrew is called Armageddon.

Notice deception goes out to the whole world including the kings of the world. At that point, Satan is allowed to deceive the nations. We will look at this further, but by now we can start to see that the infamous battle of Armageddon is not a literal battle but a gathering of evil against the Lord's people. All these enemies of the Lord are destroyed by the second coming of Christ.

Conclusion

So, all these passages present a period of tribulation and unrestrained evil. This evil period is associated with the release of Satan from the bottomless pit. At this point, though, there are still many unanswered questions, including why "forty-two months," "1260 days," and "a time, times, and half a time," describe the time between the first and second comings of Christ. I ask for your patience. We will be returning to Revelation again and will address that question then.

Also, notice I have not said how long this final tribulation will last. You may have heard of the seven-year tribulation, but nowhere does the Bible state the length of the final tribulation. For now, understand there is a period of great distress for the Church just before Jesus returns—but Jesus returns victorious and grants his people a share in the victory.

Summary

The signs of great tribulation, wide-scale apostasy, and the final Antichrist come together in Satan's little season, which will occur when Satan is no longer bound. When God removes Satan's restraints, the enemy will reveal the man of lawlessness and bring severe tribulation to the people of God, the Church.

Chapter 6

ARMAGEDDON

We ended the previous chapter on Satan's little season with the sixth bowl of wrath in Revelation 16. At the end of the time of tribulation, the forces of evil and unregenerate humanity will be united in opposition to God and his church. This passage presents a final conflict before the return of Christ. This is popularly known as the battle of Armageddon. Many see Armageddon as a reference to the ancient city of Megiddo, which is north of Jerusalem (Tel Megiddo today), where there is a great plain near the Jezreel Valley. Many significant Old Testament battles occurred at the mount and surrounding valley.

Judges 4–5 contains the story of Deborah. The Canaanite king, Jabin, and his general, Sisera, oppressed Israel; however, Deborah and Barak led God's people to victory at Megiddo. In Judges 6 the Midianites and Amalekites are camped in the Valley of Jezreel. The Lord uses Gideon and his small army to defeat them. Also, Saul and Jonathan met the Philistines at Jezreel in their military campaigns described in 1 Samuel 29–30. In 2 Kings 23:29–30, the Egyptians killed King Josiah at Megiddo. Because of these events, Revelation 16:16 reminds us of great battles of the Old Testament.

Unfortunately, because so many fail to recognize the symbolic language of Revelation, they look for another literal battle on this plain where the nations of the world will gather. Dispensationalists understand this to be a battle between the earthly nation of Israel and her enemies from the north. This misses the point, though. The imagery of Armageddon, echoing the conflicts of the Old Testament, is, as Sam Storms says, a "lasting symbol for the cosmic eschatological battle between good and evil."[33] This last battle is the culmination of the period of great tribulation against the church.

Old Testament Prophecies

This description of the climactic battle is not limited to the New Testament. We also find references to this in Old Testament prophecy. For example, Joel writes that when Jerusalem is restored, the nations will come against it in the valley of Jehoshaphat:

> For behold, in those days and at that time, when I restore the fortunes of Judah and Jerusalem, I will gather all the nations and bring them down to the Valley of Jehoshaphat. And I will enter into judgment with them there, on behalf of my people and my heritage Israel, because they have scattered them among the nations and have divided up my land, and have cast lots for my people, and have traded a boy for a prostitute, and have sold a girl for wine and have drunk it. (Joel 3:1–3)

God will bring the nations together so that he may bring judgment against them. In Zechariah 14 the Lord says he will gather all nations to Jerusalem to fight against it, but he will come and fight for Jerusalem. Ezekiel 38:16–39:5 contains prophecies against Gog from the land of Magog, the chief prince of Meshech and Tubal. This is a figure who represents one who leads those in opposition to God and believers. At the end of this section in Ezekiel 39:1–5, God comes in judgment to destroy evil:

> And you, son of man, prophesy against Gog and say, Thus says the Lord GOD: Behold, I am against you, O Gog, chief prince of Meshech and Tubal. And I will turn you about and drive you forward, and bring you up from the uttermost parts of the north, and lead you against the mountains of Israel. Then I will strike your bow from your left hand, and will make your arrows drop out of your right hand. You shall fall on the mountains of Israel, you and all your hordes and the peoples who are with you. I will give you to birds of prey of every sort and to the beasts of the field to be devoured. You shall fall in the open field, for I have spoken, declares the Lord GOD.

---

33   Storms, *Kingdom Come*, 432.

Also, this language is similar to what we find in the book of Revelation. In fact, Gog is mentioned in Revelation 20:8. So, the Old Testament foresees a time when the enemies of God are arrayed against God and his people, but God defeats these enemies once and for all.

New Testament Prophecies

The New Testament gives us a more complete description of the defeat of the enemies of Christ.

Revelation

Revelation gives us the clearest picture of this final battle. Returning to Revelation 16:12–16, notice verse 14 says the demonic spirits will gather the kings of the whole world for battle. However, something is missing in the ESV translation. The Greek does not say "assemble them for battle" but rather "assemble them for *the* battle." The word "the" is not included in the ESV translation. This is unfortunate as every other major English translation includes the word "the." For example, look at the same verse in the CSB:

> For they are demonic spirits performing signs, who travel to the kings of the whole world to assemble them for *the* battle on the great day of God, the Almighty. (Revelation 16:14, CSB)

Including the word "the" before battle is important because this is not the only place in Revelation that mentions "the battle." It is also found in Revelation 19:17–19:

> Then I saw an angel standing in the sun, and with a loud voice he called to all the birds that fly directly overhead, "Come, gather for the great supper of God, to eat the flesh of kings, the flesh of captains, the flesh of mighty men, the flesh of horses and their riders, and the flesh of all men, both free and slave, both small and great." And I saw the beast and the kings of the earth with their armies gathered to make war against him who was sitting on the horse and against his army.

Verse 19 should read, "And I saw the beast and the kings of the earth with their armies gathered to make *the* war against him who was sitting on the horse and against his army." In this instance, most English translations drop the word "the" in this verse, but it is there in the Greek. Also, look at Revelation 20:7–8:

> And when the thousand years are ended, Satan will be released from his prison and will come out to deceive the nations that are at the four corners of the earth, Gog and Magog, to gather them for battle; their number is like the sand of the sea.

Verse 8 should say "to gather them for *the* battle." Of the primary English translations, only the NASB and LSB include the word "the." So, three times Revelation refers to "the battle" or "the war." This is another strong argument for the parallel visions of the book of Revelation, but, for our purposes, what we see is a final climatic battle presented to us in three different ways.

What happens at this battle? Whereas the sixth bowl in Revelation 16:12–16 is the final battle, the seventh bowl in Revelation 16:17–21 gives us the results of this battle:

> The seventh angel poured out his bowl into the air, and a loud voice came out of the temple, from the throne, saying, "It is done!" And there were flashes of lightning, rumblings, peals of thunder, and a great earthquake such as there had never been since man was on the earth, so great was that earthquake. The great city was split into three parts, and the cities of the nations fell, and God remembered Babylon the great, to make her drain the cup of the wine of the fury of his wrath. And every island fled away, and no mountains were to be found. And great hailstones, about one hundred pounds each, fell from heaven on people; and they cursed God for the plague of the hail, because the plague was so severe.

Here we have apocalyptic language that demonstrates the finality and severity of the victory of Christ over the unbelieving world. Physical destruction and judgment fall upon the nations. "Babylon the great" refers to the world system of riches, luxury, and seduction, and the next chapter, Revelation 17, describes her fall. We also see the judgment upon wicked people represented by the plague of hail.

Now let's look at Revelation 19:17–21 for another perspective:

> Then I saw an angel standing in the sun, and with a loud voice he called to all the birds that fly directly overhead, "Come, gather for the great supper of God, to eat the flesh of kings, the flesh of captains, the flesh of mighty men, the flesh of horses and their riders, and the flesh of all men, both free and slave, both small and great." And I saw the beast and the

kings of the earth with their armies gathered to make war against him who was sitting on the horse and against his army. And the beast was captured, and with it the false prophet who in its presence had done the signs by which he deceived those who had received the mark of the beast and those who worshiped its image. These two were thrown alive into the lake of fire that burns with sulfur. And the rest were slain by the sword that came from the mouth of him who was sitting on the horse, and all the birds were gorged with their flesh.

Chapter 19 presents not only the destruction of the ungodly but also depicts the beast and the false prophet being thrown into the lake of fire. All the wicked, small and great, are slain by the sword of Jesus, the rider on the white horse. Who are the beast and false prophet? They were introduced in chapter 13 of Revelation.

Beast from the Sea

Chapter 12 begins a new vision where the dragon, Satan, looks to devour a child that will be born, and this child is Jesus. However, the dragon is defeated by the blood of the Lamb and is thrown to the earth where he pursues the woman who gave birth. This woman represents the Church, the true Israel. At the end of chapter 12, the dragon is standing on the shore of the sea. The dragon's two helpers then come on the scene in the next chapter. The beast is described in Revelation 13:1–4:

And I saw a beast rising out of the sea, with ten horns and seven heads, with ten diadems on its horns and blasphemous names on its heads. And the beast that I saw was like a leopard; its feet were like a bear's, and its mouth was like a lion's mouth. And to it the dragon gave his power and his throne and great authority. One of its heads seemed to have a mortal wound, but its mortal wound was healed, and the whole earth marveled as they followed the beast. And they worshiped the dragon, for he had given his authority to the beast, and they worshiped the beast, saying, "Who is like the beast, and who can fight against it?"

The description of this beast is similar to the beasts of Daniel 7. There the beasts represent the Babylonian, Medo-Persian, Greek, and Roman empires. Likewise, the beast in Revelation 13 represents world governments. The world governments bring persecution to the church and, during that last tribulation period, silence the church. Revelation 13:10 says,

> If anyone is to be taken captive,
>   to captivity he goes;
> if anyone is to be slain with the sword,
>   with the sword must he be slain.
> Here is a call for the endurance and faith of the saints.

Beast from the Earth

There is another beast, though, described in Revelation 13:11–18:

> Then I saw another beast rising out of the earth. It had two horns like a lamb and it spoke like a dragon. It exercises all the authority of the first beast in its presence, and makes the earth and its inhabitants worship the first beast, whose mortal wound was healed. It performs great signs, even making fire come down from heaven to earth in front of people, and by the signs that it is allowed to work in the presence of the beast it deceives those who dwell on earth, telling them to make an image for the beast that was wounded by the sword and yet lived. And it was allowed to give breath to the image of the beast, so that the image of the beast might even speak and might cause those who would not worship the image of the beast to be slain. Also it causes all, both small and great, both rich and poor, both free and slave, to be marked on the right hand or the forehead, so that no one can buy or sell unless he has the mark, that is, the name of the beast or the number of its name. This calls for wisdom: let the one who has understanding calculate the number of the beast, for it is the number of a man, and his number is 666.

The second beast is different from the first, but they work together. This beast represents false religion. The picture refers to the beast calling fire down from heaven, which reminds us of Elijah, the prophet who called down fire from heaven in front of the false prophets of Israel. This is why Revelation 19 calls this beast the false prophet. Therefore, false religion works with world governments to persecute God's people.

What about 666? What does this number represent? First, this number is not a literal mark on the hand or the forehead, and it is not your Social Security number—or any other government-issued number.

Let's take a look at how the number six is used in the Bible. Six is one short of the perfect seven. Also, at creation, it is the day God created man. So, three sixes may represent man putting himself in the place of God. This is what happened in the Fall in Genesis 3. What about the mark on the hand or the forehead? Again, we need to turn to Scripture. Where else do we find references to the hand or the forehead? Several passages from Exodus and Deuteronomy specifically reference such symbols (Exodus 13:8–9, 14–15; Deuteronomy 11:18). One is Deuteronomy 6:4–9:

> Hear, O Israel: The LORD our God, the LORD is one. You shall love the LORD your God with all your heart and with all your soul and with all your might. And these words that I command you today shall be on your heart. You shall teach them diligently to your children, and shall talk of them when you sit in your house, and when you walk by the way, and when you lie down, and when you rise. You shall bind them as a sign on your hand, and they shall be as frontlets between your eyes. You shall write them on the doorposts of your house and on your gates.

This passage refers to the hand and the forehead. The context shows Moses was not literally expecting the people to put something on their hand or forehead (although after the exile this became a common practice in certain parts of Judaism). The passage shows God's Word was to guide a person and their household. The same holds true for us. God's Word should guide what we do, as represented by the hand. It should also guide how we think, as represented by the forehead. Therefore, 666 means we recognize those who belong to the beast by how they live and how they think.

The beast from the sea represents world governments, and Revelation 13:10 shows us we need endurance and patience to withstand this beast's persecution. The beast from the earth represents false religion, and Revelation 13:18 teaches us that we need wisdom to defend against this beast's deception. Taken together, the dragon, the beast, and the false prophet are a counterfeit trinity.

Destruction of Evil

Fortunately, this counterfeit trinity is doomed. In Revelation 19:19–21 the beast and the false prophet are thrown into the lake of fire. This is a picture of the destruction of Satan's partners in opposing God. There will be no more world governments to persecute God's people, and there will be no more false religion to deceive them either.

But what about the dragon (Satan)? Revelation 20:7–10 presents the demise of Satan in the last battle:

> And when the thousand years are ended, Satan will be released from his prison and will come out to deceive the nations that are at the four corners of the earth, Gog and Magog, to gather them for battle; their number is like the sand of the sea. And they marched up over the broad plain of the earth and surrounded the camp of the saints and the beloved city, but fire came down from heaven and consumed them, and the devil who had deceived them was thrown into the lake of fire and sulfur where the beast and the false prophet were, and they will be tormented day and night forever and ever.

All the forces of evil are surrounding God's people—but God consumes them with fire. The point is not whether the fire is literal or figurative. The point is all evil is destroyed, and Satan is thrown into the lake of fire. All the passages about "the battle" describe the destruction of wickedness and evil. The destruction of wicked people is the perspective of the battle given in Revelation 16. In Revelation 19 the emphasis is on the destruction of the beast and the false prophet, and in Revelation 20 it is on the destruction of Satan. The return of Christ results in the complete elimination of all evil. (In the next chapter I will explain why this is a problem for premillennialism.[34])

The destruction of the wicked is described in other visions of Revelation without reference to a battle, such as the sixth seal in Revelation 6:12–17 and the seventh trumpet in Revelation 11:15–18:

> When he opened the sixth seal, I looked, and behold, there was a great earthquake, and the sun became black as sackcloth, the full moon became like blood, and the stars of the sky fell to the earth as the fig tree sheds its winter fruit when shaken by a gale. The sky vanished like a scroll that is being rolled up, and every mountain and island was removed from its place. Then the kings of the earth and the great ones and the generals and the rich and the powerful, and everyone, slave and free, hid themselves in the caves and among the rocks of the mountains, calling to the mountains and rocks, "Fall on us and hide us from the face of him who is seated on the throne, and from the wrath of the Lamb, for the great day of their wrath has come, and who can stand?" (Revelation 6:12–17)

---

34   See chapter 7, "The Millennium."

Then the seventh angel blew his trumpet, and there were loud voices in heaven, saying, "The kingdom of the world has become the kingdom of our Lord and of his Christ, and he shall reign forever and ever." And the twenty-four elders who sit on their thrones before God fell on their faces and worshiped God, saying,

> "We give thanks to you, Lord God Almighty,
>> who is and who was,
> for you have taken your great power
>> and begun to reign.
> The nations raged,
>> but your wrath came,
>> and the time for the dead to be judged,
> and for rewarding your servants, the prophets and saints,
>> and those who fear your name,
>> both small and great,
> and for destroying the destroyers of the earth." (Revelation 11:15–18)

The end of the fourth vision in Revelation 14:17–20 gives us another perspective:

Then another angel came out of the temple in heaven, and he too had a sharp sickle. And another angel came out from the altar, the angel who has authority over the fire, and he called with a loud voice to the one who had the sharp sickle, "Put in your sickle and gather the clusters from the vine of the earth, for its grapes are ripe." So the angel swung his sickle across the earth and gathered the grape harvest of the earth and threw it into the great winepress of the wrath of God. And the winepress was trodden outside the city, and blood flowed from the winepress, as high as a horse's bridle, for 1,600 stadia.

Revelation presents the final conflict between God and his enemies, ending with their complete defeat and destruction.

Other New Testament Passages

There are also other passages in the New Testament that show the demise of evil. For example, Paul assures the saints of it in 2 Thessalonians 1:3–10:

We ought always to give thanks to God for you, brothers, as is right, because your faith is growing abundantly, and the love of every one of you for one another is increasing. Therefore we ourselves boast about you in the churches of God for your steadfastness and faith in all your persecutions and in the afflictions that you are enduring. This is evidence of the righteous judgment of God, that you may be considered worthy of the kingdom of God, for which you are also suffering—since indeed God considers it just to repay with affliction those who afflict you, and to grant relief to you who are afflicted as well as to us, when the Lord Jesus is revealed from heaven with his mighty angels in flaming fire, inflicting vengeance on those who do not know God and on those who do not obey the gospel of our Lord Jesus. They will suffer the punishment of eternal destruction, away from the presence of the Lord and from the glory of his might, when he comes on that day to be glorified in his saints, and to be marveled at among all who have believed, because our testimony to you was believed.

Paul starts this passage by talking about the faith and love of the Thessalonian church in the face of their persecutions and afflictions. Because of these persecutions and afflictions, God is just to judge those afflicting them. This will happen when Jesus returns and inflicts vengeance on the wicked. The persecutors will go away to eternal destruction. In 2 Thessalonians 2:8 the same thing happens to the man of lawlessness:

And then the lawless one will be revealed, whom the Lord Jesus will kill with the breath of his mouth and bring to nothing by the appearance of his coming.

In Hebrews 12:25–29 God says he will shake the earth and the heavens in order to eliminate the corruption of the creation:

See that you do not refuse him who is speaking. For if they did not escape when they refused him who warned them on earth, much less will we escape if we reject him who warns from heaven. At that time his voice shook the earth, but now he has promised, "Yet once more I will shake not only the earth but also the heavens." This phrase, "Yet once more," indicates the removal of things that are shaken—that is, things that have been made—in order that the things that cannot be shaken may remain. Therefore let us be grateful for receiving a kingdom that cannot be shaken, and thus let us offer to God acceptable worship, with reverence and awe, for our God is a consuming fire.

Our God is a consuming fire. He will destroy all evil and remove everything that is not a part of his kingdom.

Summary

A final battle is coming that is, in reality, not a battle at all. We are not looking for armies gathered on a field in Israel. The area around Mount Megiddo is large, but it could not hold all the armies of the earth. The language in Revelation 16:12–16 is symbolic language for universal opposition to God and his people. Sam Storms quotes the historic premillennialist Eckhard Schnabel to summarize the true meaning of the battle of Armageddon:

> The battle of Armageddon brings the final defeat of the evil forces that rebel against God and resist Jesus Christ. It is not an actual military battle in Israel. A literal fulfillment would have been theoretically possible in the first century when armies fought on horses with swords and spears and arrows. However, even then it would have been impossible to picture all the people of the earth assembled at Megiddo in the Jezreel Valley in order to wage war against God's people, not to mention that Old Testament prophecies expected the final battle to take place in Jerusalem and on Mount Zion. The final battle of history is the destruction of the political, cultural, and religious systems of the world (the Beast and the false prophet) that opposed God and the defeat of the ungodly who refuse to follow Jesus (the Lamb). This last battle takes place when Jesus returns for the final judgment. Jesus wins the final victory of human history—not with military might, but with the word of God.[35]

The key is that last sentence where Schabel says Jesus wins the victory, not with military might, but with the Word of God. Schabel is alluding to the picture of Jesus we see in Revelation 19:11–16:

---

35 Eckhard Schnable, *40 Questions about the End Times* (Grand Rapids, MI: Kregle, 2011), 237, quoted in Storms, *Kingdom Come*, 435.

Then I saw heaven opened, and behold, a white horse! The one sitting on it is called Faithful and True, and in righteousness he judges and makes war. His eyes are like a flame of fire, and on his head are many diadems, and he has a name written that no one knows but himself. He is clothed in a robe dipped in blood, and the name by which he is called is The Word of God. And the armies of heaven, arrayed in fine linen, white and pure, were following him on white horses. From his mouth comes a sharp sword with which to strike down the nations, and he will rule them with a rod of iron. He will tread the winepress of the fury of the wrath of God the Almighty. On his robe and on his thigh he has a name written, King of kings and Lord of lords.

The name of the one on the white horse is "The Word of God." From his mouth comes a sharp sword that strikes down the nations. This is a picture of Jesus as the embodiment of the Word of God speaking the Word of God in order to destroy the enemies of God. As Hebrews 4:12 says, "For the word of God is living and active, sharper than any two-edged sword." Never underestimate the power of God's Word, for through it God created all that is, sustains all that is, regenerates all who are his, and conquers all that would come against him. The Word of God wins the final battle.

Chapter 7

THE MILLENNIUM

We now come to the millennium—the word used to categorize most of the end-time views. The word *millennium* comes from the Latin words *mille*, meaning one thousand, and *annus*, meaning year. Elaborate theologies have developed based on Revelation 20's mention of this thousand-year period. To a large degree, how you understand the one thousand years of Revelation 20:1–10 shapes your overall eschatology. We will briefly examine each of the views of the millennium. First, let's read the passage itself:

> Then I saw an angel coming down from heaven, holding in his hand the key to the bottomless pit and a great chain. And he seized the dragon, that ancient serpent, who is the devil and Satan, and bound him for a thousand years, and threw him into the pit, and shut it and sealed it over him, so that he might not deceive the nations any longer, until the thousand years were ended. After that he must be released for a little while. Then I saw thrones, and seated on them were those to whom the authority to judge was committed. Also I saw the souls of those who had been beheaded for the testimony of Jesus and for the word of God, and those who had not worshiped the beast or its image and had not received its mark on their foreheads or their hands. They came to life and reigned with Christ for a thousand years. The rest of the dead did not come to life until the thousand years were ended. This is the first resurrection. Blessed and holy is the one who shares in the first resurrection! Over

such the second death has no power, but they will be priests of God and of Christ, and they will reign with him for a thousand years. And when the thousand years are ended, Satan will be released from his prison and will come out to deceive the nations that are at the four corners of the earth, Gog and Magog, to gather them for battle; their number is like the sand of the sea. And they marched up over the broad plain of the earth and surrounded the camp of the saints and the beloved city, but fire came down from heaven and consumed them, and the devil who had deceived them was thrown into the lake of fire and sulfur where the beast and the false prophet were, and they will be tormented day and night forever and ever.

"One thousand years" is mentioned six times in those ten verses. My goal is not to provide a detailed exegesis of the passage but to show how it fits in the book of Revelation and the rest of Scripture.

There are two basic ways to approach the millennium. The first is to see it as a future time event, as pre- and postmillennialists do. The second approach is to understand the millennium as the period between the first and second comings of Christ. This is amillennialism.[36]

The binding of Satan in verse 2 means Satan cannot stop the spread of the gospel. However, just before the return of Christ, Satan will persecute the church intensely. So, in this chapter, I want to go back and defend the belief that the one thousand years of Revelation 20 refers to the time between the first and second comings of Christ, rather than solely a future period.

First, though, let's consider the other millennial theologies. The "pre" and the "post" of premillennialism and postmillennialism refer to the relationship between the return of Christ and the millennium. Premillennialists believe Jesus will return before the millennium. Postmillennialists believe Jesus will return afterward.

It is worth noting that amillennialists also believe Jesus will return after the millennium, but a difference exists. Postmillennialism looks to the future for the millennium to begin, whereas amillennialism considers the whole gospel age itself to be the millennium. Following each millennial view, I will offer a critique from an amillennial perspective.

---

36 There are postmillennialists who agree the millennium is the time between the first and second advent of Christ but diverge on other issues. I will address this in the section on postmillennialism.

Premillennialism

Premillennialism has two forms: historic and dispensational. When many Christians hear "premillennialism," they think only of dispensational premillennialism. While that view has a significant following, it is a relatively young theory; it has only been around for about two hundred years. Both historic and dispensational premillennialists approach the book of Revelation from a futurist perspective, believing Revelation 4–22 describes events that have yet to occur.

Historic Premillennialism

Historic premillennialism originated in the early church. The second-century apologist Justin Martyr believed the return of Christ would begin a one-thousand-year period of peace and righteousness on the earth. Other early teachers shared this view. An early church document, *The Epistle of Barnabas*,[37] proclaims that, after the initial six days of creation, there were to be six days of one thousand years each. The millennium is the seventh day and would occur six thousand years after creation. Primarily due to the influence of Augustine, historic premillennialism faded from view until the time of the Reformation in the sixteenth century. Also, early premillennialism was rejected because many of its adherents held to excessive literalism, and some went to the other extreme by allegorizing or spiritualizing the promises of the millennium. During the Reformation, premillennial teaching was revived by the Anabaptists, who held to some extreme end-time beliefs.[38] While dispensational premillennialism is a popular evangelical view, there are a significant number of historic premillennialists today.[39]

For example, let me summarize historic premillennialist George Eldon Ladd's (1911–1982) understanding of historic premillennialism:

1. There will be a time of great tribulation for God's people with the opposition led by the Antichrist.
2. Christ returns at the end of the period of tribulation (Revelation 19:11–16). He comes to destroy the Antichrist, Satan, and death.

---

37 *The Epistle of Barnabas* was written between AD 70 and 132 and is referenced by many early church fathers. While some considered the epistle authoritative, most church fathers did not consider it divinely inspired but accepted it as a valuable historical document.

38 See Timothy George, *Theology of the Reformers*, revised edition (Nashville: B&H Publishing, 2013), 270–71, for examples.

39 Venema, *The Promise of the Future*, 195–98.

3. However, the destruction of evil and death is progressive. Revelation 19:17–21 describes the destruction of the Antichrist and those who supported him during the period of great tribulation. Revelation 20 then describes the destruction of Satan.

4. There are two stages to the demise of Satan.

    a. Satan is bound in the bottomless pit for one thousand years. While bound, he can no longer deceive the nations as he did through the Antichrist (Revelation 20:1–3). Associated with the binding of Satan is the "first resurrection" of believers. These resurrected believers will rule with Christ on this earth for one thousand years (Revelation 20:5).

    b. After one thousand years Satan is released and leads the unregenerate in a final rebellion against God. The final battle occurs, and Satan and his followers are defeated. Satan is cast into the lake of fire (Revelation 20:4–6). Associated with Satan's defeat is a second resurrection of the dead that were not part of the first resurrection (Revelation 20:5).

5. Then comes the final judgment. Those not found written in the book of life are cast into the lake of fire along with Death and Hades.

6. Once all sin and evil have been banished, the eternal state begins.[40]

There are other important aspects of historic premillennialism.

1. The one thousand years may or may not be literal.
2. The millennium will be a period of peace and prosperity even though sin exists.
3. God has one people consisting of redeemed Jews and Gentiles. The one people of God reign with Christ during the millennium.
4. Believers are resurrected and judged before the millennium.
5. Unbelievers are resurrected and judged after the millennium.

Dispensational Premillennialism

Dispensational premillennialism is a newer view of the millennium that came to prominence in the nineteenth century. One of the core beliefs of classic dispensationalism is the distinction made between Israel and the Church. God has two plans, one for the Church and one for the nation of Israel. This is important because dispensationalists believe God

---

40 George Eldon Ladd, "Historic Premillennialism," in *The Meaning of the Millennium: Four Views*, ed. Robert G. Clouse (Downers Grove, IL: InterVarsity Press, 1977), 17–18. Also, see Appendix A, "End Times Charts," for an overview of historic premillennialism.

will resume his plan for Israel during the millennium. Today many dispensationalists in academia are progressive dispensationalists. They still see a separation between the Church and Israel with God fulfilling his promises to Israel during the millennium. Ultimately, however, all the people of God, Jew or Gentile, will share in the same blessings in the new heavens and new earth.

Understanding the kingdom of God is key to dispensational premillennialism. Whereas amillennialism views the kingdom of God as a spiritual kingdom that will be realized in its fullness in the new heavens and new earth when Jesus returns, dispensational premillennialism requires a literal, physical kingdom on the current earth with the Davidic king on the throne.[41] According to dispensationalists, that is what God promised to Israel in the Old Testament. During his earthly ministry, Jesus offered the kingdom to the Jews, but they rejected it. Therefore, God suspended his kingdom plan for Israel and turned to the Church. (The Church is a "mystery" or "secret" form of the kingdom.) The kingdom promised to Israel will be realized during the millennium, when Jesus reigns on the throne in Jerusalem.

Here is a summary of dispensationalist Charles Ryrie's (1925–2016) description of dispensational premillennialism:

1. The rapture of the Church (1 Thessalonians 4:13–18; 1 Corinthians 15:51–57; John 14:1–3) will occur before the start of the seven-year tribulation.[42] The rapture consists of:
   a. The descent of Christ for his church.
   b. The resurrection of the New Testament believers that have died.
   c. The bodies of those alive at the rapture will be transformed into immortal bodies.
   d. The resurrected believers and those alive at that time will ascend to heaven.
   e. The believers now in heaven will face the judgment seat of Christ (2 Corinthians 5:10) where their works will be judged. This will result in reward or loss of reward (1 Corinthians 3:11–15).
2. The great tribulation will follow the rapture.
   a. The tribulation will be for seven years, as this is the fulfillment of the seventieth week of Daniel (Daniel 9:27).[43]

---

41 See chapter 3, "The Kingdom of God."
42 This is the most prevalent view among premillennialists; however, some believe the rapture will occur at the midpoint of the tribulation, and some believe the rapture will occur after the tribulation.
43 See chapter 13, "The Seventy Weeks."

b.   The tribulation will consist of judgment of the world (Revelation 6; 8–9; 16), persecution of Israel (Matthew 24:9, 22; Revelation 12:17), salvation for many (Revelation 7), and the rise and rule of the Antichrist (2 Thessalonians 2; Revelation 13).

3.   At the end of the tribulation, Satan gathers the nations for the battle of Armageddon, and Christ wins complete victory over Satan and his followers (Revelation 19).

a.   The resurrection of the just occurs (Luke 14:14; John 5:28–29). This is the first resurrection (Revelation 20:5) and includes those who were saved and died during the tribulation (Revelation 20:4) and the Old Testament saints (Daniel 12:2).

b.   The judgment of the Gentiles occurs in the valley of Jehoshaphat when Christ returns (Joel 3:2). These are the Gentiles alive when Christ returns after the tribulation. They are judged based on how they treated Israel. Each person is either saved and enters the millennial kingdom or is cast into the lake of fire (Matthew 25:31–46).

c.   The judgment of Israel—Jews who are alive when Christ returns after the tribulation—occurs on the earth. Those who accepted the Messiah enter the millennial kingdom; those who did not are lost (Ezekiel 20:37–38).

4.   The millennium begins after the post-tribulation return of Christ (Revelation 20:1–6). It is a one-thousand-year earthly reign of Christ which fulfills the Abrahamic, Davidic, and New Covenant.

a.   The millennium is also called the kingdom of heaven (Matthew 6:10), the kingdom of God (Luke 19:11), the kingdom of Christ (Revelation 11:15), the regeneration or "new world" (Matthew 19:28), the times of refreshing (Acts 3:19–20), and the world to come (Hebrews 2:5).

b.   Christ as king will rule from Jerusalem (Revelation 19:16; Isaiah 2:3), and his reign will result in peace, equity, justice, prosperity, and glory (Isaiah 11:2–5).

c.   During the millennium Satan is bound (powerless). He will remain bound until the end of the millennium; at which time he will be released.

5.   After the millennium Satan will deceive the nations by leading them in a final rebellion against Christ. This will result in Satan being defeated and cast by God into the lake of fire (Revelation 20:7–10).

6.   The resurrection of the unjust occurs. All those not saved from the Fall onward will be raised (Revelation 20:12).

a.   The unjust stand before God at the Great White Throne judgment. They are before the Great White Throne because they rejected Christ, and their works show they deserve eternal punishment. Those not written in the book of life (which is everyone present) are cast into the lake of fire (Revelation 20:11–15).

b.   The judgment of fallen angels occurs. They are judged because they followed Satan in his rebellion. All are cast into the lake of fire (Jude 6; 1 Corinthians 6:3).

7.   The eternal state begins.[44]

There are other aspects of dispensational premillennialism not mentioned by Ryrie.

1.   During the great tribulation, the Antichrist makes a covenant with Israel but breaks that covenant halfway through the seven years. He stops sacrifices occurring at a temple that was rebuilt sometime before the rapture of the Church.

2.   During the millennium, sacrifices are occurring at either the same temple or another temple based on the temple described in Ezekiel.[45]

3.   Some dispensationalists believe the distinctions between Israel and other nations, and Israel and the Church, continue into the eternal state.[46]

---

44   Charles C. Ryrie, "A Synopsis of Bible Doctrine," *Ryrie Study Bible* (Chicago: Moody Press, 1995), 2075–77. Also, see Appendix A, "End Times Charts", for an overview of dispensational premillennialism.

45   See chapter 14, "Ezekiel's Temple."

46   Dispensationalist Mark A. Snoeberger states, "We find that the eternal state will feature the subsumption of the kingdoms of the whole earth under the universal reign of God the Father (1 Cor 15:28). This fact does not mean … that the nations of the earth will simply disappear. Instead, the closing chapters of the Revelation indicate that historical nations will persist into the eternal state, and further, that they will continue their pattern of streaming to the new Jerusalem (Rev 21:24, 26; 22:2). The reason they will do this … is that they will enjoy here the continued priestly services of the Jewish nation, which retains a distinctive place among the nations forever (so Rev 21:12)." Mark A. Snoeberger, "Traditional Dispensationalism," in *Covenantal and Dispensational Theologies: Four Views on the Continuity of Scripture*, eds. Brent E. Parker and Richard J. Lucas (Downers Grove, IL: InterVarsity Press, 2022), 178–79. Later in that passage, Snoeberger states, "For the dispensationalist, Israel is neither replaced by the church nor typical of the church (though analogies may be drawn between them), and neither is it a growing aggregate that expands to include the church. Israel and the church remain distinct forever."

Premillennial Issues

Now that we have the basics of both forms of premillennialism, let's consider the weaknesses in their argument. This will not be comprehensive as I have already addressed problems with premillennialism, especially dispensational premillennialism, in other chapters, and I will also be addressing premillennialism in future chapters.

Improper Hermeneutics

The first problem for both types of premillennialism is allowing the millennium in Revelation 20 to drive the interpretation of other passages. The one thousand years mentioned there are found nowhere else in Scripture. There are two other references to one thousand years in the Bible.[47] The first is in Psalm 90:3–4:

> You return man to dust
> and say, "Return, O children of man!"
> For a thousand years in your sight
> are but as yesterday when it is past,
> or as a watch in the night.

The second reference is in 2 Peter 3:8:

> But do not overlook this one fact, beloved, that with the Lord one day is
> as a thousand years, and a thousand years as one day.

None of these other references to one thousand years apply directly to Revelation 20:1–10, and 2 Peter 3:8 even seems to argue against the one thousand years in Revelation being a literal one thousand years. In addition, the premillennialist view applies many of God's Old Testament promises to Israel to the millennium, claiming the millennium is when those promises will be fulfilled.[48] However, no clear link between any Old Testament passage and the one thousand years of Revelation exists. There are certainly links between Old Testament passages and judgment, but there is no reason to look for prophecies of restoration to be fulfilled in a future millennium. Sam Storms writes,

---

47 Ecclesiastes 6:6 also references one thousand years, but not one thousand years from God's perspective.
48 See chapter 3, "The Kingdom of God."

Rather than reading ... texts through the grid of Revelation 20, the latter should be read in the clear light of the former. Sound hermeneutical procedure would call on us to interpret the singular and obscure in the light of the plural and explicit. To make the rest of the New Testament (not to mention the Old Testament) bend to the standard of one text in the most controversial, symbolic, and by scholarly consensus most difficult book in the Bible is hardly commendable hermeneutical method. We simply must not allow a singular apocalyptic tail to wag the entire epistolary dog! We must not force the whole of Scripture to dance to the tune of Revelation 20.[49]

Multiple Returns

The second problem with dispensational premillennialism specifically is the belief Christ will return more than once. The main reason for rejecting two returns of Christ, and thus the millennium in between, is the New Testament presents the return of Christ as the *telos*, or end or goal, of all things.[50]

Chronology

The third problem with premillennialism is the belief Revelation 20 chronologically follows Revelation 19. If the events in chapter 20 follow the events of chapter 19, then we must conclude there is a one-thousand-year period after the return of Christ. However, chapter 19 clearly presents the return of Christ in victory and glory. The enemies of God are destroyed when Christ returns.[51] This is found multiple times in Revelation.

- There is the "great day of their wrath" for the great and small on the earth (Revelation 6:12–17).
- God's wrath comes and the dead are judged (Revelation 11:15–18).
- There is the "great winepress of the wrath of God" Revelation 14:17–20).
- God makes Babylon "drain the cup of the wine of the fury of his wrath" (Revelation 16:17–21).

Chapter 19 goes even further in describing the victory of Christ. Look closely at verses 17–18:

---

49 Storms, *Kingdom Come*, 557–58.
50 See chapter 4, "The Return of Christ."
51 See chapter 6, "Armageddon."

> Then I saw an angel standing in the sun, and with a loud voice he called
> to all the birds that fly directly overhead, "Come, gather for the great
> supper of God, to eat the flesh of kings, the flesh of captains, the flesh of
> mighty men, the flesh of horses and their riders, and the flesh of *all men*,
> both free and slave, both small and great."

The birds are to feast on kings, captains, mighty men, horses with their riders, and *all men, both free and slave, both small and great.* No one is excluded. Furthermore, verse 21 says, "And the rest were slain by the sword that came from the mouth of him who was sitting on the horse, and all the birds were gorged with their flesh." Everyone that might possibly be left is destroyed. Finally, the beast and the false prophet are thrown into the lake of fire (v. 20).

Therefore, when Revelation 20:1–3 says Satan is bound for one thousand years so he can no longer deceive the nations, if chapter 20 follows chapter 19 chronologically, what nations are these? All the people and nations were destroyed at the end of chapter 19, which parallels the earlier descriptions of the end and parallels the demise of Satan and the final judgment in Revelation 20:11–15. The internal evidence of Revelation does not allow chapter 20 to chronologically follow chapter 19. Chapter 20 is the beginning of a new vision within the book of Revelation.

Evil and Death

Finally, a significant problem for premillennialism is there is evil and death after the return of Christ. According to premillennialism, during the millennial reign of Christ, there will be sin and death culminating with the rebellion led by Satan after his release from the abyss. However, not only will there be evil and death in the millennium, but resurrected believers in their incorruptible, resurrected bodies will live alongside the unregenerate with un-resurrected, corruptible bodies. Further, this means believers with incorruptible bodies will be living on a still corruptible earth. The primary chapter on the resurrection of our bodies, 1 Corinthians 15, does not allow for this mixture of incorruptible and corruptible. Look at 1 Corinthians 15:42–44:

> So is it with the resurrection of the dead. What is sown is perishable;
> what is raised is imperishable. It is sown in dishonor; it is raised in glory.
> It is sown in weakness; it is raised in power. It is sown a natural body;
> it is raised a spiritual body. If there is a natural body, there is also a
> spiritual body.

The resurrection body is imperishable, glorious, powerful, and spiritual. (Spiritual does not mean immaterial, but completely empowered by the Holy Spirit.) Furthermore, the resurrection of the body means there is no more death. According to 1 Corinthians 15:50,

> I tell you this, brothers: Flesh and blood cannot inherit the kingdom of God, nor does the perishable inherit the imperishable.

Note that "flesh and blood cannot inherit the kingdom of God," yet premillennialists claim the millennium is the realization of the kingdom of God. Now, a premillennialist would claim that the unregenerate during the millennium are not part of the kingdom of God. However, what follows verse 50 does not allow for any person who is still susceptible to sin and death to be present on the earth. Continuing after verse 50, we see the perishable body is now imperishable, and the mortal body is now immortal (v. 53). Note the timing, though, in verse 54: "*When* the perishable puts on the imperishable, and the mortal puts on immortality, *then* shall come to pass the saying that is written: 'Death is swallowed up in victory.'" The significance of this is clear. Once the resurrection occurs, death is powerless. Death doesn't just end for the resurrected believers; death is eliminated (swallowed up in victory). If there is no death, then there can be no sin (v. 57). Therefore, a future millennium on a corruptible earth still susceptible to sin and death after the return of Christ and the resurrection cannot be.

Conclusion

There are other problems with premillennialism, especially dispensational premillennialism, but the key difficulty is allowing Revelation 20 to guide our interpretation of the rest of the Bible. When we do, we necessarily have Christ returning more than once, people with imperishable bodies living alongside people with perishable bodies, and evil and death continuing after the return of Christ.

Postmillennialism

What we know of today as postmillennialism comes from the Puritans. John Owen in England and Jonathan Edwards in America were both postmillennialists. Into the nineteenth and early twentieth centuries, postmillennialism was the predominant view at Princeton, including such men as A. A. Hodge, Charles Hodge, and B. B. Warfield. The early to mid-twentieth century saw a decline in postmillennialism.[52] However, there was

---

52 Venema, *The Promise of the Future*, 222–23.

a resurgence of postmillennialism beginning in the late twentieth century, which has continued into the twenty-first century.

Here is a summary of postmillennialist Lorraine Boettner's (1901–1990) description of postmillennialism.

1. The kingdom of God is currently being expanded throughout the world through the preaching of the gospel and the power of the Holy Spirit.

2. The world will eventually be Christianized, and Christ will return after an extended period of righteousness and peace, which is the millennium.

3. The general resurrection, the judgment of all people, and the new heavens and new earth all follow the return of Christ.

4. The millennium will be a golden age of prosperity during the present era of the Church and will last for an extended period, maybe much longer than one thousand years.

5. Because of the influence of the gospel, all aspects of life—social, economic, political, and cultural—will be greatly improved.

6. Not everyone will be a Christian, and sin will still be present. However, the various forms of evil will be negligible. Christian principles will be the norm.[53]

Advocates of postmillennialism insist the triumph of the gospel and the millennium before the return of Christ are necessary implications of Christ's universal dominion as King. Those who advocate other millennial views that do not see the triumph of the gospel before the return of Christ are guilty of unbiblical pessimism. Christ's current reign at the Father's right hand must be expressed on the earth before Christ returns, so other millennial views are denying Christ's present reign. Postmillennialism agrees with amillennialism that Christ has a spiritual kingdom, but for the postmillennialist, Christ's kingdom will be seen on the current earth as well.

Theonomy and Reconstructionism

An offshoot of mainstream postmillennialism is the postmillennialism espoused by reconstructionists and theonomists. They advocate for applying the Old Testament moral and civil law to modern society. Cornelis Venema explains it like this:

---

53 Lorraine Boettner, "Postmillennialism," in *The Meaning of the Millennium: Four Views*, ed. Robert G. Clouse (Downers Grove, IL: InterVarsity Press, 1977), 117–18. Also, see Appendix A, "End Times Charts," for an overview of postmillennialism.

According to the chief representatives of this movement, the dominion of Christ will come to expression in history by way of the reconstruction of society according to biblical norms and laws. Christ's millennial reign in history requires that Christian believers seek to bring all aspects of life—not only ecclesiastical, but also familial, economic, social, political, etc.—under the lordship of Jesus Christ. In the public square as much as in the private, the explicit principles and teachings of the Word of God must and will direct the affairs of the nations. Their terminology of 'theonomy' is used to insist that the biblical laws, including the Old Testament case laws and their prescribed capital punishments for various offences (adultery, homosexuality, idolatry, disobedience to parents) be honoured and applied in exhaustive detail by governments today. The same laws, including the judicial laws, that were set forth for the governance of Israel, the Old Testament people of God in the days of the theocracy, should also be held out today as the standard for governments and their judicial instruments.[54]

As an example, consider this quote from theonomist David Chilton in his book *Productive Christians in an Age of Guilt Manipulators*:

We have seen that worldwide blessing is promised in Christ; that when He came He was victorious; that His victory continues throughout the earth as His kingdom expands; and that the expansion of His kingdom follows the fearless delivery of the gospel into all nations .... It should be clear that the reign of Christ in the hearts and social structures of men will produce responsibility and freedom under the law of God. As men mature in this responsibility and freedom, they will be granted more (Matthew 25:21, 23). With increased work, savings, and capital investment, productivity will rise, creating more capital for investment, and so on. *There will be uninterrupted growth over time until the Last Day*, and poverty will disappear. Those who remain ungodly will be disinherited, as God's providential forces in history work against them. The wealth of the sinner is laid up for the just (Proverbs 13:22). God's people will inherit *land* as we

---

54 Venema, *The Promise of the Future*, 228–29.

mature, as we submit ourselves to biblical law and extend its implications all through society.[55]

Therefore, theonomists and reconstructionists see the golden age to come not just as a golden age for the gospel but also an age of global prosperity living under God's Old Testament moral and civil law.

Christian Nationalism

Today, some postmillennialists advocate for Christian nationalism. Christian nationalism has proven difficult to define, but Paul Miller from Georgetown University gives this definition:

> Christian nationalism asserts that there is something identifiable as an American "nation," distinct from other nations; that American nationhood is and should remain defined by Christianity or Christian cultural norms; and that the American people and their government should actively work to defend, sustain, and cultivate America's Christian culture, heritage, and values.[56]

Generally speaking, a Christian nationalist believes the government should be Christian. This means the government should promote Christianity and Christian values. However, this does not mean that all those who seek to bring about changes in laws are themselves Christian nationalists. They may simply be attempting to establish laws that reflect biblical standards. For example, the pro-life movement is filled with Christians praying and working to abolish abortion. Therefore, a person is not a Christian nationalist simply because they desire laws that conform to God's moral law. However, it is beyond my scope to analyze the movement in its entirety.[57] The point is that Christian nationalism meshes well with postmillennialism.

---

55 David Chilton, *Productive Christians in an Age of Guilt Manipulators* (Tyler, TX: Institute for Christian Economics, 1981), 241 (emphasis original).

56 Paul D. Miller, *The Religion of American Greatness: What's Wrong with Christian Nationalism* (Downers Grove, IL: IVP Academic, 2022), 4, quoted in Tom Ascol, *The Perils and Promises of Christian Nationalism* (Cape Coral, FL: Founders Press, 2023), 8.

57 See John D. Wilsey, "The Many Faces of Christian Nationalism," *Law & Liberty*, September 26, 2022, for the historical background to Christian nationalism, including Puritan postmillennialism.

"Amillennial" Postmillennialists

The heading of this section is a tongue-in-cheek reference to postmillennialists who do not anticipate a future millennium. Along with amillennialists, these postmillennialists agree the one thousand years of Revelation 20 represent the gospel age, the time between the first and second advent of Christ. If this is the case, why not call amillennialists "postmillennialists," or call these postmillennialists "amillennialists"? The postmillennialism that Keith Mathison presents in his book *Postmillennialism: An Eschatology of Hope* cannot be called amillennialism for several reasons, but I'll just mention two:

1. His approach to Revelation differs significantly from typical amillennialism. There is much agreement with amillennialism on Revelation 20, but the chapters preceding are viewed from a preterist perspective. This means that, in his view, Revelation 6–19 describes the judgment of Jerusalem in AD 70.[58] However, amillennialists approach Revelation from an idealist perspective.[59]

2. The understanding of the kingdom of God differs from amillennialism. According to Mathison, Christ's kingdom is a spiritual kingdom, but it is also realized on the current earth in the current age. Christ's reign and authority extend to the earthly nations.[60] However, the postmillennial kingdom is much different from the premillennial kingdom. Postmillennialists such as Mathison do not expect to see Jesus ruling on a throne in Jerusalem. Also, the realization of the kingdom on this earth does not necessarily result in a golden age of peace and prosperity. Amillennialists, on the other hand, view the present kingdom as a spiritual kingdom with the fullness of the kingdom being realized on the new earth after Jesus returns.[61]

This form of postmillennialism is not compatible with theonomy or Christian nationalism. It is most concerned with the expansion of the kingdom of God under Christ in all nations.[62] Let me summarize Mathison's presentation of postmillennialism.

---

58   Keith A. Mathison, *Postmillennialism: An Eschatology of Hope* (Phillipsburg, NJ: P&R Publishing, 1999), 155.
59   See chapter 1, "The Ground Rules."
60   Mathison, *Postmillennialism*, 180.
61   See chapter 3, "The Kingdom of God."
62   Mathison, *Postmillennialism*, 190.

1. Christ's kingdom was inaugurated at his first coming. He is ruling in hearts by the Holy Spirit, and he is ruling the nations.

2. Satan is bound, so the millennium extends from the first coming to the second coming of Christ.

3. Christ's kingdom is primarily redemptive.

4. Christ's kingdom will fill the whole earth before he returns. The growth of the kingdom is progressive, and Satan's kingdom does not grow in parallel to Christ's kingdom.

5. Christ's kingdom grows through the power of the Holy Spirit. This is accomplished through the ordinary means of preaching, sacraments, and worship. Even though the kingdom does not come through politics, national governments are under Christ's kingdom. According to Mathison, "Postmillennialism renounces all political or earthly attempts to further the messianic kingdom and relies solely upon the supernatural work of God."[63]

6. There will be a large-scale conversion to Christ across the earth before Christ returns. Christ's kingdom "will reach a point where the majority of men and nations have willingly submitted to Jesus the Messiah."[64]

7. Christ's kingdom will only be fully consummated when he returns.[65]

So, there are some similarities between Mathison's version of postmillennialism and amillennialism, with the primary difference being the current nature of Christ's kingdom.

Postmillennial Issues

What amillennialists find most objectionable about postmillennialism is the idea of a golden age—an age in which the world is Christianized and there is a long period of righteousness and peace. Given that Jesus said the gospel would be "proclaimed throughout the whole world as a testimony to all nations" (Matthew 24:13), and there will be a multitude "from every nation, from all tribes and peoples and languages, standing before the throne and before the Lamb" (Revelation 7:9), why would amillennialists disagree with postmillennialists over a golden age in the future?

---

63 Mathison, *Postmillennialism*, 193.
64 Mathison, *Postmillennialism*, 193.
65 Mathison, *Postmillennialism*, 190–94.

Kingdom Parables

The first reason I reject this future golden age is Jesus's teaching about the kingdom. In Matthew 13:31–33 Jesus gives two short parables that describe God's kingdom:

> He put another parable before them, saying, "The kingdom of heaven is like a grain of mustard seed that a man took and sowed in his field. It is the smallest of all seeds, but when it has grown it is larger than all the garden plants and becomes a tree, so that the birds of the air come and make nests in its branches." He told them another parable. "The kingdom of heaven is like leaven that a woman took and hid in three measures of flour, till it was all leavened."

The small mustard seed sprouts and becomes a tree that is larger than all the other plants in the garden. The leaven spreads throughout the whole measure of flour. Both of these short parables proclaim the gospel starts small but expands throughout the earth. However, these two parables are sandwiched between Jesus's presentation of the parable of the weeds in Matthew 13:24–30 and his explanation of the parable of the weeds in Matthew 13:36–43. In that parable, the kingdom of heaven is like a man who sowed good seed in his field, but an enemy came and sowed weeds among the wheat. When the wheat began to sprout, the weeds appeared. The servants asked the master why the field has weeds when only wheat was sown. The master replied that an enemy had sown the weeds. The servants wanted to remove the weeds, but the master did not allow it because removing the weeds would disturb the wheat. Both the wheat and the weeds had to grow until the harvest when the wheat would be separated from the weeds. Later, the disciples asked Jesus to explain the parable:

> Then he left the crowds and went into the house. And his disciples came to him, saying, "Explain to us the parable of the weeds of the field." He answered, "The one who sows the good seed is the Son of Man. The field is the world, and the good seed is the sons of the kingdom. The weeds are the sons of the evil one, and the enemy who sowed them is the devil. The harvest is the end of the age, and the reapers are angels. Just as the weeds are gathered and burned with fire, so will it be at the end of the age. The Son of Man will send his angels, and they will gather out of his kingdom all causes of sin and all law-breakers, and throw them into the fiery furnace. In that place there

> will be weeping and gnashing of teeth. Then the righteous will shine like the sun in the kingdom of their Father. He who has ears, let him hear. (Matthew 13:36–43)

There is no separation between the sons of the kingdom and the sons of the evil one until Jesus returns. Also, there is no hint that as the number of the sons of the kingdom increases, the number of the sons of the evil one will decrease. Only when the Son of Man returns will he "gather out of his kingdom all causes of sin and all law-breakers, and throw them into the fiery furnace."[66]

Suffering and Persecution

The second reason I do not see a future golden age is there is no biblical indication the suffering and persecution that follow the spread of the gospel will abate. In Lystra Paul was stoned, dragged out of the city, and left for dead. However, the Lord raised him up and he and Barnabas went to Derbe. We read in Acts 14:21–22,

> When they had preached the gospel to that city and had made many disciples, they returned to Lystra and to Iconium and to Antioch, strengthening the souls of the disciples, encouraging them to continue in the faith, and saying that through many tribulations we must enter the kingdom of God.

After preaching in Derbe, Paul returned to Antioch, passing through Lystra and Iconium. He encouraged the new believers to remain faithful, but he also ensured they knew tribulations would come. In 2 Timothy 3:10–13, Paul recalls these events:

> You, however, have followed my teaching, my conduct, my aim in life, my faith, my patience, my love, my steadfastness, my persecutions and sufferings that happened to me at Antioch, at Iconium, and at Lystra—which persecutions I endured; yet from them all the Lord rescued me. Indeed, all who desire to live a godly life in Christ Jesus will be persecuted, while evil people and impostors will go on from bad to worse, deceiving and being deceived.

---

66   This point parallels the signs of tribulation, apostasy, and antichrist discussed in chapter 5, "The Return of Christ." Those signs are ongoing throughout the gospel age.

Paul reiterates his warning that the godly in Christ will be persecuted, and the ungodly will not move toward godliness but toward even more ungodliness. His warning of persecution echoes what Jesus said in John 16:33:

> I have said these things to you, that in me you may have peace. In the world you will have tribulation. But take heart; I have overcome the world.

There is no indication Paul's or Jesus's warnings and encouragements will no longer apply as the gospel spreads. While we rejoice in the spread of the gospel, it does not result in a golden age. Suffering and persecution continue until Jesus returns. Postmillennialists acknowledge that sin continues until the end, but there is no indication in Scripture that the expansion of Christ's kingdom will reduce the opposition to Christ's kingdom.

Sanctification

The third reason I do not see a golden age presented in the Bible is the need for sanctification. Sanctification is a vital part of the Christian life. No evidence of sanctification in a person's life indicates there was likely no previous regeneration or justification. Lack of growth in a person who claims to be in Christ is often confirmation the person is not really in Christ. However, even if there was a great outpouring of the Holy Spirit, and a vast majority of people alive today were truly born again and granted faith in Christ, that would not eliminate the need for sanctification. Every new believer needs discipleship and time to grow in Christ. To be clear, postmillennialists do not deny that sanctification is needed and will occur. However, one of the primary ways God sanctifies us is through suffering and trial. If our lives are free of trouble, then a vital means of sanctification is lost.[67]

There must be opposition for us to properly mature in Christ. As 1 Peter 1:6–7 says, we need trials to test our faith:

> In this you rejoice, though now for a little while, if necessary, you have been grieved by various trials, so that the tested genuineness of your faith—more precious than gold that perishes though it is tested by fire—

---

67 Note that in the "Christian" West, the lack of persecution has not led to a growth in Christian influence, but a loss of it. Secularization is on the march. This is not a reason to reject postmillennialism, but simply an observation for consideration.

> may be found to result in praise and glory and honor at the revelation of
> Jesus Christ.

Trials refine our faith as gold is refined in the fire. We should want our faith to "result in praise and glory and honor at the revelation of Jesus Christ." Furthermore, as James wrote, we need trials to make us "perfect and complete, lacking in nothing":

> Count it all joy, my brothers, when you meet trials of various kinds, for
> you know that the testing of your faith produces steadfastness. And let
> steadfastness have its full effect, that you may be perfect and complete,
> lacking in nothing. (James 1:2–4)

Also, we need the hope that results from suffering as Paul said in Romans 5:1–5:

> Therefore, since we have been justified by faith, we have peace with
> God through our Lord Jesus Christ. Through him we have also obtained
> access by faith into this grace in which we stand, and we rejoice in hope
> of the glory of God. Not only that, but we rejoice in our sufferings, know-
> ing that suffering produces endurance, and endurance produces charac-
> ter, and character produces hope, and hope does not put us to shame,
> because God's love has been poured into our hearts through the Holy
> Spirit who has been given to us.

This kind of hope comes from the character built by enduring suffering. This hope "does not put us to shame" (or "disappoint us" as the CSB translates it) because the Holy Spirit pours out God's love into our hearts. Suffering does not make us question God's love, but God uses suffering to affirm his love for us.

Blessing

Next, I reject a golden age because persecution brings blessings. Jesus said in Matthew 5:10–12,

> Blessed are those who are persecuted for righteousness' sake, for theirs
> is the kingdom of heaven. Blessed are you when others revile you and
> persecute you and utter all kinds of evil against you falsely on my account.
> Rejoice and be glad, for your reward is great in heaven, for so they perse-
> cuted the prophets who were before you.

Persecution is a blessing because it is a sign we belong to Christ's kingdom. We are to rejoice when persecuted because we will be rewarded in heaven. As Peter said in 1 Peter 3:14, "But even if you should suffer for righteousness' sake, you will be blessed."

Opposition

Finally, I reject a golden age because of the level of opposition the church will encounter before Christ returns. The major opposition against the Church once Satan is released indicates there are many who are still unregenerate. Revelation 20:7–9 says,

> And when the thousand years are ended, Satan will be released from his prison and will come out to deceive the nations that are at the four corners of the earth, Gog and Magog, to gather them for battle; their number is like the sand of the sea. And they marched up over the broad plain of the earth and *surrounded the camp of the saints and the beloved city*, but fire came down from heaven and consumed them.

Satan and the wicked nations *surround* the Church. Even though the Church is not literally surrounded, the word picture cries out overwhelming opposition. The situation is dire, so Christ will be even more glorified in the victory. Great opposition against God's people is for God's glory. Consider the Exodus from Egypt. After the Israelites left Egypt, Pharoah determined to pursue because God had hardened his heart. The Israelites are trapped between the Red Sea and Pharoah's army. The people cried out that it would have been better to stay slaves in Egypt. God led his people to this place and then ensured Pharoah would come after them. Why would God do this? So he would get the glory. Look at Exodus 14:15–18:

> The LORD said to Moses, "Why do you cry to me? Tell the people of Israel to go forward. Lift up your staff, and stretch out your hand over the sea and divide it, that the people of Israel may go through the sea on dry ground. And I will harden the hearts of the Egyptians so that they shall go in after them, and *I will get glory* over Pharaoh and all his host, his chariots, and his horsemen. And the Egyptians shall know that I am the LORD, when *I have gotten glory* over Pharaoh, his chariots, and his horsemen."

God's people are surrounded and threatened, so he will be glorified in the deliverance. We see something similar in 2 Chronicles 13. There, Abijah, the king of Judah, goes out to battle against Jeroboam, the king of Israel. Judah is outnumbered two to one. Abijah has 400,000 soldiers, and Jeroboam has 800,000 soldiers. Abijah warns Jeroboam not to fight against Judah because they will be fighting against the Lord. However, Jeroboam has his much larger army surround Abijah's army. But "God defeated Jeroboam and all Israel before Abijah and Judah" (2 Chronicles 13:15). Five hundred thousand men of Israel fell in battle. As verse 18 says, "Thus the men of Israel were subdued at that time, and the men of Judah prevailed, because they relied on the LORD, the God of their fathers." Overwhelming opposition is a prime occasion for the Lord to display his glory and power.

Therefore, the biblical evidence is there will be many who are hostile toward God's people before Christ returns. As Kim Riddlebarger says, "Though postmillenarians do believe in a great apostasy before Christ's return, this does not sufficiently explain how the present evil age could be completely transformed by the kingdom of God only to become essentially evil again during the brief period of apostasy."[68]

Conclusion

Jesus's teaching on the kingdom of heaven does not leave room for a golden age. The Bible promises no decline in suffering, trials, and persecution for those who belong to Christ, and God uses these difficulties to mature our faith. Without trials and persecution, we lose a means of blessing for now and eternity. Finally, Christ will be glorified when he destroys the evil surrounding his church when he returns. For these reasons, I reject the postmillennialists' assertion of a future golden age resulting from the spread of the gospel.

Amillennialism

Amillennialism is in a different category from premillennialism and some forms of post-millennialism because amillennialists are not looking for a future millennium. The time between the first and second comings of Christ is the "one thousand years" spoken of in Revelation 20. This is why it has the name *amillennialism*. The "a" signifies negation (for example, an *anomaly* is something that is not the norm). Therefore, amillennialism literally means "no millennium." This is a bit of a misnomer because amillennialism recognizes the one thousand years as referring to a real time period, but not in the future and certainly not exactly one thousand years. Other names for amillennialism have been suggested, but no other name is likely to replace the term. The primary assertions of amillennialism are

---

68 Riddlebarger, *A Case for Amillennialism*, 300n35. Excerpt from *A Case for Amillennialism* by Kim Riddlebarger, copyright © 2013. Used by permission of Baker Books, a division of Baker Publishing Group.

1. The millennium is now. It extends from the first coming of Christ to the second coming of Christ.
2. The signs of the times, such as opposition to the gospel, tribulation, apostasy, and antichrist, are both present and future realities.
3. The binding of Satan refers to Satan's inability to stop the spread of the gospel.
4. Satan will bring severe persecution against the church sometime just before the return of Christ when he is no longer restrained.
5. There will be one general bodily resurrection of believers and unbelievers when Christ returns.
6. There will be one judgment of believers and unbelievers when Christ returns.
7. Satan and all evil along with all unbelievers will spend eternity in the lake of fire, which is hell.
8. Christ will establish the new heavens and new earth as the eternal dwelling place with his people.
9. Christ will not return multiple times or in multiple stages. Rather, it will be a single return in which he wraps up all of history.

Answering Objections to Amillennialism

We can ascertain the objections to amillennialism from our discussion of the problems with premillennialism and postmillennialism. I'll just list a few of them since I have already discussed some objections:

1. The amillennial view of Revelation consisting of parallel visions is not correct since Revelation should be read as a sequence of events from chapter 4 onward. Most other objections follow from this one.
2. Chapter 20 follows chapter 19 both sequentially and chronologically.
3. Amillennialism does not hold to a literal one thousand years.
4. The binding of Satan results in a complete restriction of Satan's activity on the earth.
5. Revelation 20 teaches two bodily resurrections instead of one bodily resurrection.

Objections two, three, and four are probably the most problematic teachings of amillennialism to premillennialists. I addressed objection two earlier in this chapter, and I addressed objection four in chapter 5, "Satan's Little Season." I will address objection five in chapter 8. Objection three is interesting because it ignores Revelation's genre. Why should one thousand years in Revelation 20 be taken literally? A better question is, "Why should any number in Revelation be considered literal?" The numbers in Revelation give meaning, not statistical information. This is why translations that convert distances in Revelation to modern-day measurements lose meaning instead of enhancing meaning. For example, Revelation 14:20 refers to 1,600 stadia:

> And the winepress was trodden outside the city, and blood flowed from the winepress, as high as a horse's bridle, for 1,600 stadia.

However, the CSB translates it as "180 miles" instead of 1,600 stadia.[69] While 180 miles is understandable as a distance for the modern-day reader, 180 miles has no meaning other than 180 miles. Yes, 180 miles is a long distance, but the actual idea that is being communicated is missing. Four is the number associated with the earth, as in the four corners of the earth, and ten represents completeness. The number 1,600 is 4 x 4 x 10 x 10, which indicates the judgment of the world is complete. Also, in like manner, many numbers in other parts of Scripture must be taken symbolically. For example, we see a reference to "a thousand hills" in Psalm 50:10:

> For every beast of the forest is mine,
> the cattle on a thousand hills.

No one interprets "a thousand hills" as literally one thousand hills. Why not? Because the Psalms are poetry, and to understand "a thousand hills" as literally one thousand hills would obscure the meaning. So, if that is the case, why in a book such as Revelation that is full of symbolism would we require the one thousand years to be literally one thousand years? Understanding one thousand years (10 x 10 x 10) as a period of completeness gives us greater insight into the actual meaning of the passage.

Pessimistic or Optimistic?

Some postmillennialists object that amillennialism is pessimistic since amillennialists do not see a bright future, a golden age. To restate, while the Bible clearly proclaims the gospel will spread across the entire world (Matthew 24:14; Revelation 5:9; 7:9), the Bible also shows persecution follows the spread of the gospel (John 15:18–21; 1 Peter 4:12–14). There are reprieves from tribulation in societies heavily influenced by Christianity, but those pauses in persecution are temporary.

---

69   The CSB does give the literal translation of "1,600 stadia" in a footnote to the verse. The NASB 1995 has "two hundred miles" with "sixteen hundred stadia" listed in a footnote, but the NASB 2020 says "1,600 stadia."

I don't consider amillennialism pessimistic because the Bible presents a hopeful future. While persecution and suffering continue until the end, other than the brief time when Satan is released, the gospel continues to move forward in power. Trials for the Church do not mean Satan's kingdom is expanding. Only God's kingdom expands. The Church through the power of the Word and the Spirit plunders Satan's realm so that in the end there will be "a great multitude that no one could number, from every nation, from all tribes and peoples and languages, standing before the throne and before the Lamb" (Revelation 7:9). That is the truly optimistic message of the Bible.

Summary

I have sought to demonstrate that amillennialism is the most appropriate way to understand biblical eschatology. Even though I hold to amillennialism confidently, I do so in humility. Proponents of other views hold the Scripture in high regard and are seeking to be faithful to Scripture as I am. I simply disagree with their approach to Scripture. In his book *Kingdom Come: An Amillennial Alternative*, Sam Storms provides an excellent summary of the strengths of amillennialism.

1. Amillennialism best accounts for the Bible's teaching on the kingdom of God. The kingdom of God is a present reality in the Spirit and will be consummated at the return of Christ. The kingdom is not pushed off to a future millennium.[70]

2. Amillennialism best accounts for the one thousand years of Revelation 20. The one thousand years represents the time between the first and second comings of Christ.

3. Amillennialism gives a better understanding of the seventy weeks of Daniel 9. The ten jubilees are symbolic of the work of redemption, which results in the final jubilee—the new heavens and new earth.[71]

4. Amillennialism sees the return of Christ as the end of physical death.

5. Amillennialism does not have resurrected and non-resurrected bodies existing together on the earth.

6. Amillennialism understands the promises to Israel to be fulfilled in the Church, the true Israel of God. Historic premillennialists also believe this, but this makes a future millennium unnecessary.[72]

---

70 See chapter 3, "The Kingdom of God."
71 See chapter 13, "The Seventy Weeks."
72 See chapter 1, "The Ground Rules."

7. Amillennialism has no place for a rebuilt temple or the resumption of animal sacrifices.[73]

8. Amillennialism alone accounts for why Satan must be bound in the first place. Premillennialism says Satan will be bound from deceiving nations that were already defeated and destroyed at the end of chapter Revelation 19. It makes no sense to say Revelation 20 tells us God will protect nations from Satan's deception after the nations have already been deceived by Satan and then destroyed by the return of Christ.[74]

9. Amillennialism states that there will be one general resurrection and one final judgment.[75]

10. Amillennialism best uses the hermeneutical principle of the analogy of faith, which is that Scripture interprets Scripture. The interpretation of Revelation 20 is guided by the rest of Scripture instead of Revelation 20 guiding the interpretation of much of Scripture.[76]

---

73 See chapter 14, "Ezekiel's Temple."
74 See chapter 5, "Satan's Little Season."
75 See chapter 8, "The General Resurrection," and chapter 9, "The Final Judgment."
76 Storms, *Kingdom Come*, 549–57.

Chapter 8

THE GENERAL RESURRECTION

Part of the glorious message of the Christian gospel is the resurrection of Christ. His bodily resurrection from the grave demonstrated the Father's acceptance of his sacrifice. On top of that, his resurrection also guarantees the resurrection of all who are in Christ.

The doctrine of the resurrection of the body is vital to Christianity. Pagan religions see no hope or future for the body after death, but, as Christians, we have great hope for both our physical bodies and our eternal souls. The early heresy of Gnosticism viewed matter as evil and spirit as good. The goal was to be free of the confines of the body. Christianity refutes this. The body is just as important as the soul. Jesus became flesh. He took on a body that died and was then resurrected, not discarded. Jesus, in his death, not only redeemed our souls, but he also redeemed our bodies.

Body and soul belong together. The soul is not more important than the body, and the body is nothing without the soul. At death, we enter the intermediate state: the souls of unbelievers go to a place of torment, while the souls of believers go to be with the Lord. Both Christians and non-Christians are conscious and aware during this intermediate state. However, the final state includes both the soul and body. The final state of the unbeliever is the body and soul together in hell, the lake of fire. The final state of the believer is body and soul together in the presence of God in heaven, which is the new heavens and new earth. For body and soul to be together in the future state, the body must be raised from the grave, glorified (removing the effects of sin), and reunited with the soul. This reunion occurs at the general resurrection when Christ returns. It is called a general resurrection because both believers and unbelievers are resurrected together at Christ's return.[77]

One Resurrection

Premillennialism, on the other hand, requires more than one resurrection to take place. Both historic and dispensational premillennialists believe those in Christ will be resurrected at the beginning of the millennium, and unbelievers will be resurrected at the end. Dispensational premillennialists also add two more resurrections. The four resurrections in order are

1. The initial resurrection of believers will occur at the rapture, before the seven-year tribulation period.

2. Another resurrection must happen after the seven-year tribulation (before the start of the millennium) for those who came to Christ and died during the tribulation.

3. A third resurrection comes at the end of the millennium for saints who died during the millennium.

4. The fourth resurrection is the resurrection of all unbelievers at the end of the millennium.[78]

I will later make the case that the dispensational understanding of the rapture and the seven-year tribulation is incorrect,[79] and I have already explained that their understanding of the millennium is flawed.[80]

So why address this issue here? First, we need to have confidence in our understanding of the resurrection of the body; and second, I want to show the importance of not having our theology drive our interpretation of the Bible. The Bible presents one worldwide resurrection of all who are in the grave. This occurs at the singular return of Christ. Separate resurrections for believers and unbelievers are not found in Scripture. Let's look at some Scriptures that present one general resurrection.

The one general resurrection of believers and unbelievers is first found in the Old Testament. Job writes he will see his Redeemer in his flesh, even after his flesh has been destroyed,

---

77   My focus is not on the resurrection body of the believer, but on the number of bodily resurrections associated with the second advent of Christ.

78   Hoekema, *The Bible and the Future*, 239.

79   See chapter 13, "The Seventy Weeks."

80   See chapter 7, "The Millennium."

> For I know that my Redeemer lives,
>   and at the last he will stand upon the earth.
> And after my skin has been thus destroyed,
>   yet in my flesh I shall see God,
> whom I shall see for myself,
>   and my eyes shall behold, and not another. (Job 19:25–27)

Job is referring to his resurrection. However, Daniel expands our understanding, proclaiming it is a resurrection of all people:

> At that time shall arise Michael, the great prince who has charge of your people. And there shall be a time of trouble, such as never has been since there was a nation till that time. But at that time your people shall be delivered, everyone whose name shall be found written in the book. And many of those who sleep in the dust of the earth shall awake, some to everlasting life, and some to shame and everlasting contempt. And those who are wise shall shine like the brightness of the sky above; and those who turn many to righteousness, like the stars forever and ever. (Daniel 12:1–3)

The end of Daniel 11 is a prophecy of an antichrist-type figure, and Daniel 12 reveals this antichrist figure will bring great trouble for God's people. However, there will be a resurrection of those who are dead. Some of those resurrected will be raised to eternal life and some to everlasting destruction, but it is clear that the righteous and the unrighteous will be resurrected at the same time.

Turning to the New Testament, John records Jesus's words about a single resurrection:

> Do not marvel at this, for an hour is coming when all who are in the tombs will hear his voice and come out, those who have done good to the resurrection of life, and those who have done evil to the resurrection of judgment. (John 5:28–29)

All who are in the tombs will come out. Some will be resurrected to life and others to judgment. Dispensationalists claim there are one thousand years between the resurrection of life and the resurrection of judgment, but there is nothing in the text here or elsewhere that supports a one-thousand-year gap. Dispensationalists rely on stretching the meaning of the word "hour" to add one thousand years between the two resurrections. They allow "hour" in verse 28 to span one thousand years because verse 25 also mentions an "hour":

> Truly, truly, I say to you, an hour is coming, and is now here, when the dead will hear the voice of the Son of God, and those who hear will live.

Jesus says an hour is coming and is already here when those who hear the voice of the Son will live. Jesus is referring to regeneration. In regeneration, we are brought from death to life. This "hour" has now lasted over two millennia. The dispensationalists argue that if the "hour" in verse 25 can last over two thousand years, why can't the "hour" in verse 28 represent one thousand years? This is quite a stretch because it ignores how John uses the word "hour." There are times when John uses the word "hour" he is referring to an extended period of time. For example, consider John 4:23:

> But the hour is coming, and is now here, when the true worshipers will worship the Father in spirit and truth, for the Father is seeking such people to worship him.

In Jesus's conversation with the woman at the well, he does not mean true worshipers will only worship for one literal hour while he talks with the woman. Jesus is referring to the New Testament age. However, there are many instances in the Gospel of John in which the word "hour" refers to a specific moment or event in time. Sometimes this point in time has not yet arrived, as in John 7:30 where he writes, "So they were seeking to arrest him, but no one laid a hand on him, because his hour had not yet come." Other times when John uses "hour," he is referring to a point in time that has arrived. John 12:20–23 demonstrates this:

> Now among those who went up to worship at the feast were some Greeks. So these came to Philip, who was from Bethsaida in Galilee, and asked him, "Sir, we wish to see Jesus." Philip went and told Andrew; Andrew and Philip went and told Jesus. And Jesus answered them, "The hour has come for the Son of Man to be glorified."

We also read in John 13:1, "Now before the Feast of the Passover, when Jesus knew that his hour had come to depart out of this world to the Father." Therefore, we can reasonably interpret the "hour" referred to in John 5:28 as a point in time. If this "hour" were parallel to the "hour" in verse 25, which refers to the age in which we live, then there should be resurrections taking place all during the church age. Furthermore, Jesus said, "All who are in the tombs will hear his voice" (John 5:28). It is not plausible to make that refer to two different groups at two different times.[81] Rather than describing two resurrections, Jesus is presenting a single resurrection with two different outcomes.

Another passage that presents a single resurrection is Acts 24:14–15. This is part of Paul's defense before Felix:

> But this I confess to you, that according to the Way, which they call a sect, I worship the God of our fathers, believing everything laid down by the Law and written in the Prophets, having a hope in God, which these men themselves accept, that there will be a resurrection of both the just and the unjust.

Note that Paul said, "There will be *a resurrection* of *both* the just and the unjust." If Paul had said, "There will be a resurrection of the just and the unjust," you could perhaps argue there will be a resurrection of the just and a separate resurrection of the unjust. However, the word "both" is included. There will be "a resurrection of both." In other words, there will be a single resurrection of the just and the unjust. Can we call two resurrections separated by one thousand years "a resurrection"?[82] We cannot.

Premillennial Arguments

Having considered Scriptures that present a single, general resurrection, let's examine some premillennial arguments for more than one resurrection.

First, premillennialists look to Revelation 20:4–6 to prove two resurrections:

> Then I saw thrones, and seated on them were those to whom the authority to judge was committed. Also I saw the souls of those who had been beheaded for the testimony of Jesus and for the word of God, and those who had not worshiped the beast or its image and had not received its mark on their foreheads or their hands. They came to life and reigned with Christ for a thousand years. The rest of the dead did not come to life until the thousand years were ended. This is the first resurrection.

---

81 Hoekema, *The Bible and the Future*, 241.
82 Hoekema, *The Bible and the Future*, 241.

> Blessed and holy is the one who shares in the first resurrection! Over
> such the second death has no power, but they will be priests of God and
> of Christ, and they will reign with him for a thousand years.

This passage speaks of the first resurrection. Some come to life and reign with Christ during the one thousand years (first resurrection), and some come to life after the one thousand years (second resurrection). If this passage is referring to a future period, dispensationalists might have a case for two bodily resurrections since two resurrections are mentioned. However, the question is, are both resurrections bodily resurrections? The premillennialist argues if one of the resurrections is bodily, then both resurrections must be bodily. The end of verse 4 says, "They came to life and reigned with Christ for a thousand years." Is that referring to a bodily resurrection?

Yes, the first resurrection is a bodily resurrection because Jesus bodily rose from the dead in victory. All other resurrections of believers are tied to the resurrection of Christ. As 1 Corinthians 15:17–19 says,

> And if Christ has not been raised, your faith is futile and you are still in
> your sins. Then those also who have fallen asleep in Christ have per-
> ished. If in Christ we have hope in this life only, we are of all people most
> to be pitied.

Those in Christ have hope beyond this life because Christ rose from the dead. Our bodies will be resurrected because of Christ's resurrection. However, there is currently a spiritual aspect to Christ's resurrection. Jesus physically rose from the grave and all who are in him rose with him (Colossians 3:1). How do we rise with him? We initially experience the first resurrection through regeneration. Look at Ephesians 2:4–6:

> But God, being rich in mercy, because of the great love with which he
> loved us, even when we were dead in our trespasses, made us alive
> together with Christ—by grace you have been saved—and raised us up
> with him and seated us with him in the heavenly places in Christ Jesus.

Paul writes God "made us alive together with Christ." God "raised us up with" Christ. He "seated us with him in the heavenly places in Christ Jesus." What does Revelation 20:4 say? It says, "They came to life and reigned with Christ." From the words of Jesus to the letters of the apostles Paul and John, Scripture speaks clearly about the nature of this resurrection:

Truly, truly, I say to you, whoever hears my word and believes him who sent me has eternal life. He does not come into judgment, but has passed from death to life. (John 5:24)

In him also you were circumcised with a circumcision made without hands, by putting off the body of the flesh, by the circumcision of Christ, having been buried with him in baptism, in which you were also raised with him through faith in the powerful working of God, who raised him from the dead. (Colossians 2:11–12)

If then you have been raised with Christ, seek the things that are above, where Christ is, seated at the right hand of God. (Colossians 3:1)

We know that we have passed out of death into life, because we love the brothers. Whoever does not love abides in death. (1 John 3:14)

Regeneration is God making us alive. This is a spiritual resurrection.

Also note what John wrote in Revelation 20:4. Here John sees "the souls of those who had been beheaded for the testimony of Jesus and for the word of God, and those who had not worshiped the beast or its image and had not received its mark on their foreheads or their hands." Similar language is used in the fifth seal in Revelation 6:9–11:

When he opened the fifth seal, I saw under the altar the souls of those who had been slain for the word of God and for the witness they had borne. They cried out with a loud voice, "O Sovereign Lord, holy and true, how long before you will judge and avenge our blood on those who dwell on the earth?" Then they were each given a white robe and told to rest a little longer, until the number of their fellow servants and their brothers should be complete, who were to be killed as they themselves had been.

Revelation 20:4 and Revelation 6:9 both refer to the souls of martyrs for the faith. Chapter 20 goes further because it mentions the souls of those who were not martyred but remained faithful unto death. The souls under the altar in the fifth seal cry out for judgment and are told to rest until the final martyr has been killed. In chapter 20 the souls come to life and reign with Christ. When the fifth seal is opened, the souls are given a white robe. Each passage reflects different aspects of saints presently reigning with Christ while waiting for the return of Christ. Thus, the first resurrection in Revelation 20:6 represents those whose souls after physical death are with the Lord. Those who are regenerated (spiritually raised from death to life) while physically alive are the souls with Christ after death. They are alive and reigning with Christ.

Revelation 20:5 says, "The rest of the dead did not come to life until the thousand years were ended." The "rest of the dead" are unbelievers. Those who die without Christ do not experience any type of resurrection until the general resurrection when Christ returns.

Again, the premillennialists cry foul. One resurrection can't have a spiritual component and another resurrection be solely physical. However, Revelation 20:4–6 not only speaks of two resurrections; it also speaks of a second death (v. 6):

> Blessed and holy is the one who shares in the first resurrection! Over such the second death has no power, but they will be priests of God and of Christ, and they will reign with him for a thousand years. (Revelation 20:6)

The second death has no power over those who are a part of the first resurrection. If there is a future one-thousand-year reign of Christ that occurs after a physical resurrection of believers, then only those believers physically resurrected before the millennium are guaranteed to be spared from the second death. Those saved during the millennium cannot be a part of the first resurrection if the first resurrection has already occurred. There are two qualifications for being spared the second death (the lake of fire): being a part of the first resurrection (Revelation 20:6) and having your name written in the book of life (Revelation 20:15). Therefore, the first resurrection must refer to Christ's resurrection and those spiritually raised in him. It cannot be a physical resurrection of believers before the millennium.

Furthermore, everyone agrees the first death, which is implied, is physical death. Because there is the first death, our physical death, there is also a resurrection of the body. However, after the second resurrection, there is a second death. Verses 14 and 15 describe this second death:

> Then Death and Hades were thrown into the lake of fire. This is the second death, the lake of fire. And if anyone's name was not found written in the book of life, he was thrown into the lake of fire. (Revelation 20:14–15)

The second death is the lake of fire, which is hell. Note this death occurs after the resurrection of the body; therefore, the second death is spiritual since the body does not physically die again. So, there is a physical death and a spiritual death. Why then can there not be a spiritual resurrection in Christ (based on his physical resurrection) and a physical resurrection when Christ returns? If you are raised spiritually (you are born again and go to be with Christ at death), you do not die spiritually. However, if you are not raised spiritually (you are not born again and do not go to be with Christ at death), you will die spiritually. The table below shows the relationship between the two resurrections and the two deaths:[83]

Believers	Unbelievers
First (spiritual) resurrection	
First (physical) death	First (physical) death
Second (physical) resurrection	Second (physical) resurrection
	Second (spiritual) death

Next, premillennialists appeal to 1 Corinthians 15:20–25 to prove two resurrections:

But in fact Christ has been raised from the dead, the firstfruits of those who have fallen asleep. For as by a man came death, by a man has come also the resurrection of the dead. For as in Adam all die, so also in Christ shall all be made alive. But each in his own order: Christ the firstfruits, then at his coming those who belong to Christ. Then comes the end, when he delivers the kingdom to God the Father after destroying every rule and every authority and power. For he must reign until he has put all his enemies under his feet.

From this passage, they argue for three chronological stages with respect to the resurrection. First is the resurrection of Christ, referred to as "the firstfruits" (v. 20). This is the age we live in now. The second stage is "at his coming those who belong to Christ" (v. 23). This refers to the millennium. Finally, the end comes after Jesus has destroyed every rule, authority, and power (v. 24). This is the final eternal kingdom. Premillennialists claim these stages correspond to what is found in Revelation 20. Those "at his coming who belong to Christ" are those who are physically raised as part of the first resurrection men-

---

83 Adapted from Simon J. Kistemaker, *Exposition of the Book of Revelation*, New Testament Commentary (Grand Rapids, MI: Baker Books, 2001), 540. Excerpt from *Exposition of the Book of Revelation* by Simon J. Kistemaker, copyright © 2001. Used by permission of Baker Academic, a division of Baker Publishing Group.

tioned in chapter 20. However, this interpretation requires finding two resurrections in 1 Corinthians 15:20–25 when the text mentions only one resurrection ("then at his coming those who belong to Christ"). So, according to the premillennialist, this passage references the resurrection of Christ, the general resurrection, and then the final state.[84] Again, we see the backward nature of interpretation. Because Revelation 20 must refer to two bodily resurrections, the premillennialist must reject the plain interpretation of 1 Corinthians 15:20–25, which proclaims only one. George Murray said this about premillennialism seeing two bodily resurrections in Revelation 20:

> The anomaly confronting us here is that one can read the whole Bible with-
> out discovering an inkling of this doctrine [the doctrine of two resurrections
> separated by a thousand years] until he arrives at its third from the last
> chapter. If, on coming to that chapter, he shall give a literal interpretation
> to one sentence of a highly symbolical passage, he will then find it necessary
> to retrace his steps and interpret all the eschatological teachings of the Bible
> in a manner agreeable to this one sentence. The recognized rule of exegesis is
> to interpret an obscure passage of Scripture in the light of a clear statement.
> In this case, clear statements are being interpreted to agree with the literal
> interpretation of one sentence from a context replete with symbolism, the
> true meaning of which is highly debatable.[85]

Other passages that show one resurrection when Jesus returns can be found in the Gospel of John and Paul's epistles:

> For this is the will of my Father, that everyone who looks on the Son and
> believes in him should have eternal life, and I will raise him up on the last
> day. (John 6:40)

How can there be another resurrection one thousand years after the "last day"?[86] One of the arguments of the premillennialist is unbelievers are not mentioned in 1 Thessalonians 4:16 or 1 Corinthians 15:23. It is true that 1 Thessalonians 4:16 says, "The dead in Christ will rise first," and 1 Corinthians 15:23 says, "at his coming those who belong to

---

84   Venema, *The Promise of the Future*, 203–4.
85   George Murray, *Millennial Studies* (Grand Rapids, MI: Baker, 1948), 153–54, quoted in
     Hoekema, *The Bible and the Future*, 242.
86   Hoekema, *The Bible and the Future*, 243.

Christ." However, the contexts of both show that Paul is presenting the resurrection as a comfort to believers. Why mention unbelievers when unbelievers would not be comforted by the resurrection? Judgment and the lake of fire await unbelievers after the resurrection.[87] While 1 Thessalonians 4:16 does say "The dead in Christ will rise first," it does not say "The dead not in Christ will rise second." Rather, those who rise second are believers who are alive when Christ returns.

Summary

Given that the millennium is not a future event, and based on the clear teaching of the rest of Scripture, we must reject the idea of two resurrections—one for believers and another for unbelievers. The Bible presents only one resurrection. As Paul said in Acts 24:15, there will be "a resurrection of both the just and the unjust."

---

87 Hoekema, *The Bible and the Future*, 244.

Chapter 9

THE FINAL JUDGMENT

W hen Jesus returns, all who are in the grave—believers and unbelievers alike—will be raised from the dead. What happens *after* the resurrection, though? Hebrews 9:27 is perhaps the most quoted verse to show physical death is not the end of existence, and life and death are not a repeating cycle:

> And just as it is appointed for man to die once, and after that comes judgment.

Physical death happens once, and after death comes judgment. The New Testament shows this judgment occurs after the general resurrection. This is the final judgment, also known as the great white throne judgment. I call it the "final" judgment because judgment is not just limited to the end of the timeline. The Bible is clear that God has judged people and nations throughout human history and continues to do so today. God passed judgment when Adam and Eve sinned. During Noah's day, God destroyed the earth with a flood. He also wiped out Sodom and Gomorrah, passed judgment on Pharaoh and Egypt, and even sent Israel and Judah into exile because of their idolatry and disobedience. In the New Testament Ananias and Sapphira were struck down when they lied. Jerusalem and the temple were destroyed in AD 70. God continues to exercise judgment today, and he will continue to do so until Jesus returns. We read this in Romans 1:18:

> For the wrath of God is revealed from heaven against all ungodliness and unrighteousness of men, who by their unrighteousness suppress the truth.

God's wrath is presently revealed. Paul goes on to explain that God's wrath is revealed when he gives the wicked over to greater and greater sin. Yet, in Romans 2:1–5, Paul also writes that we can store up wrath for the final judgment:

> Therefore you have no excuse, O man, every one of you who judges. For in passing judgment on another you condemn yourself, because you, the judge, practice the very same things. We know that the judgment of God rightly falls on those who practice such things. Do you suppose, O man—you who judge those who practice such things and yet do them yourself—that you will escape the judgment of God? Or do you presume on the riches of his kindness and forbearance and patience, not knowing that God's kindness is meant to lead you to repentance? But because of your hard and impenitent heart you are storing up wrath for yourself on the day of wrath when God's righteous judgment will be revealed.

Simply put, intermediate judgments exist and so will a final one. Referring to the final judgment, the Apostles' Creed says, "He will come to judge the living and the dead." The "he" is Jesus; "the living" are those alive when he returns; and "the dead" are those in the grave. Jesus said the final judgment separates the sheep from the goats (Matthew 25:31–46), that is, the believers from the unbelievers. This judgment does not determine whether someone is worthy of eternity with Christ. That was settled before the foundation of the world when the names of those belonging to Christ were written in the book of life (Revelation 13:8; 17:8). The final judgment is for assigning reward and punishment. My purpose in this chapter is not to examine fully the final judgment but to show that, just as there is only one resurrection, there is also only one judgment for believers and unbelievers.

One Judgment

As with other events surrounding the return of Christ, there are disagreements over the final judgment. Premillennialism, especially dispensationalism premillennialism, anticipates several judgments that are distinguished by the place, the subjects, and the timing. This is necessitated because they believe the millennium comes at the end of human history.

A minimum of two judgments is required for all forms of premillennialism since premillennialism espouses two resurrections. The first judgment occurring at the time of the dispensational rapture is often called the *bema* seat judgment. This judgment is found in 2 Corinthians 5:10, and dispensationalists claim this judgment is only for believers:

For we must all appear before the judgment seat of Christ, so that each one may receive what is due for what he has done in the body, whether good or evil.

The Greek word for judgment in this verse is *bematos*, which comes from the Greek word *bema*, which means place of judgment. Based on their understanding of the millennium, dispensationalists claim this place of judgment is different from the great white throne of Revelation 20. However, as we established earlier, Christ returns at the end of the one thousand years, which is the age we live in now, so there can only be one final judgment. This is made clear in how the Scriptures speak of the day of judgment.

So, dispensationalism sees four judgments in Scripture. The first is the judgment of believers at the rapture. The second and third judgments are the judgment of Israel and the judgment of the nations, which both occur after the seven-year tribulation and before the millennium. The final judgment is the great white throne judgment, which takes place at the end of the millennium. This term comes from Revelation 20:11: "Then I saw a great white throne and him who was seated on it."

Old Testament Judgment

When we turn to the Old Testament, we find it speaks of the "day of the Lord" or just "the day," especially in the writings of the prophets. Sometimes the phrase "day of the Lord" refers to an intermediate judgment and sometimes to the final judgment. In Isaiah 13:6–9, "the day of the Lord" is referred to as a battle, which is the judgment of Babylon, and it promises terror and wrath. In Jeremiah 46:10, the "day of the Lord" is a devouring sword of judgment on Egypt. Ezekiel 13:5 says the false prophets have not prepared the people for the "day of the Lord." Ezekiel 30:3 describes the "day of the Lord" as a "day of clouds" and a "time of doom" for the nations. Joel references the "day of the Lord" five times. The prophet Amos uses the "day of the Lord" to refer to judgment on the northern kingdom of Israel by the Assyrians. In Obadiah the "day of the Lord" refers to judgment coming upon Edom and the nations—but it is a day that also brings salvation for the people of God. Zechariah's "day of the Lord" tells of judgment coming on Judah and the nations, yet on that day there is also refuge in the Lord for the humble. Finally, when Malachi references the "day of the Lord," he is referring to the coming of the Lord himself. The Lord brings justice, purifies worship, and takes those who are his.[88] How-

---

88   "The Day of the Lord in the Prophets," in *The ESV Study Bible* (Wheaton, IL: Crossway, 2008), 1668.

ever, even temporal judgments referenced by the "day of the Lord" prefigure—are types of—the final judgment. There is no hint in the Old Testament of multiple end-times judgments.

New Testament Judgment

The New Testament, though, brings clarity to the "day of the Lord." First, the New Testament teaches us that Jesus, in his role as Messiah, is given the authority to judge. Jesus said so in John 5:

> For the Father judges no one, but has given all judgment to the Son, that all may honor the Son, just as they honor the Father. Whoever does not honor the Son does not honor the Father who sent him. (John 5:22–23) For as the Father has life in himself, so he has granted the Son also to have life in himself. And he has given him authority to execute judgment, because he is the Son of Man. (John 5:26–27)

In Acts 17 Paul preaches to the Athenians on Mars Hill. He closes by calling them to repent, warning them of the judgment of the risen Son:

> The times of ignorance God overlooked, but now he commands all people everywhere to repent, because he has fixed a day on which he will judge the world in righteousness by a man whom he has appointed; and of this he has given assurance to all by raising him from the dead. (Acts 17:30–31)

Even though dispensationalists insist the judgment in 2 Corinthians 5:10 is a separate judgment from the great white throne judgment, it is Christ who is the judge. Therefore, the great white throne is truly Christ's judgment seat. Also, consider Matthew 25:31–32, where Jesus describes the final judgment:

> When the Son of Man comes in his glory, and all the angels with him, then he will sit on his glorious throne. Before him will be gathered all the nations, and he will separate people one from another as a shepherd separates the sheep from the goats.

When Jesus comes, he will sit on his glorious throne, his judgment seat, and pass final judgment on all people. There is no indication Jesus performs multiple "final" judgments.[89]

The description of who will face judgment also points to one final judgment. The Scriptures proclaim that every single person, those in Christ and those not in Christ, will be judged at the same time. First, consider Revelation 20:12–13:

> And I saw the dead, great and small, standing before the throne, and books were opened. Then another book was opened, which is the book of life. And the dead were judged by what was written in the books, according to what they had done. And the sea gave up the dead who were in it, Death and Hades gave up the dead who were in them, and they were judged, each one of them, according to what they had done.

These verses refer to the dead in general, and the language implies all the dead, both believers and unbelievers, will be judged at the same event. Verse 15 says, "And if anyone's name was not found written in the book of life, he was thrown into the lake of fire." Further, Romans 2:5–8 describes two categories of people at the judgment: those who seek the things of God versus those who are self-seeking:

> But because of your hard and impenitent heart you are storing up wrath for yourself on the day of wrath when God's righteous judgment will be revealed. He will render to each one according to his works: to those who by patience in well-doing seek for glory and honor and immortality, he will give eternal life; but for those who are self-seeking and do not obey the truth, but obey unrighteousness, there will be wrath and fury.

Both categories of people face "the day of wrath when God's righteous judgment will be revealed." In Matthew 25:31–33, all the nations are gathered before the throne, and Jesus separates the sheep from the goats:

> When the Son of Man comes in his glory, and all the angels with him, then he will sit on his glorious throne. Before him will be gathered all the nations, and he will separate people one from another as a shepherd

---

89   Venema, *The Promise of the Future*, 397–98.

> separates the sheep from the goats. And he will place the sheep on his
> right, but the goats on the left.

Again, there are two categories of people represented by sheep (righteous) and goats (unrighteous), and both are gathered before the judgment throne. Later, verse 46 shows the final state of each:

> And these [unrighteous] will go away into eternal punishment, but the
> righteous into eternal life.

Therefore, every single person will stand in judgment before the great white throne of God.[90] There is no indication of multiple judgments. When considered in the light of the rest of the New Testament, the primary reference for a separate judgment for believers, 2 Corinthians 5:10, does not warrant including another judgment associated with the return of Christ.

Summary

Revelation 20:11–15 is the best summary of the final judgment:

> Then I saw a great white throne and him who was seated on it. From his
> presence earth and sky fled away, and no place was found for them. And
> I saw the dead, great and small, standing before the throne, and books
> were opened. Then another book was opened, which is the book of life.
> And the dead were judged by what was written in the books, according to
> what they had done. And the sea gave up the dead who were in it, Death
> and Hades gave up the dead who were in them, and they were judged,
> each one of them, according to what they had done. Then Death and
> Hades were thrown into the lake of fire. This is the second death, the lake
> of fire. And if anyone's name was not found written in the book of life, he
> was thrown into the lake of fire.

Here, Jesus is not presented as the Lamb of God who takes away the sin of the world but as the supreme Judge. The general resurrection has already happened, and all people are standing before the throne. Both the ground and the sea are empty of bodies, and

---

90   Venema, *The Promise of the Future*, 399.

Hades and Paradise are empty of souls. All souls have been reunited with their bodies. This throng of people includes believers and unbelievers. Each person is judged by what is written in the books, that is, what they did in this life. Note, though, that works do not determine the final destination of anyone. Whether or not someone is cast into the lake of fire, which is hell, is based on whether his name is written in the book of life. If a person's name is not found in the book of life, they are sent to the lake of fire, where Death and Hades have been cast. Revelation 21:8 says,

> But as for the cowardly, the faithless, the detestable, as for murderers, the sexually immoral, sorcerers, idolaters, and all liars, their portion will be in the lake that burns with fire and sulfur, which is the second death.

However, Revelation 21:5–7 gives comfort to the believer:

> And he who was seated on the throne said, "Behold, I am making all things new." Also he said, "Write this down, for these words are trustworthy and true." And he said to me, "It is done! I am the Alpha and the Omega, the beginning and the end. To the thirsty I will give from the spring of the water of life without payment. The one who conquers will have this heritage, and I will be his God and he will be my son."

Those who hunger and thirst for righteousness will drink freely from the spring of the water of life. The conquerors in Christ are sons of God. Our ultimate hope is not in who we are or what we have done. Our ultimate hope is in whose we are. If you belong to Christ, your name was written in the book of life before the foundation of the world. While we must give an account for our life and be rewarded or suffer lack of reward based on our works, our sure hope comes from knowing we are in Christ. As our lives are examined at the great white throne judgment, we will be overwhelmed with the grace shown us in Christ.

Chapter 10

THE NEW HEAVENS AND NEW EARTH

We now come to the final major topic: the new heavens and new earth. While most Christians know the Bible teaches there will be new heavens and a new earth, our concept of what these are can be rather fuzzy. Many times, we speak of one day being in heaven without any real understanding of what that entails. For those of us who are a bit older, our theology of the new heavens and new earth may come from the hymns of our youth. Our old hymns refer to mansions, pearly gates, and streets of gold. Other people may adopt the caricature of heaven with people sitting on clouds and strumming harps. We must beware lest we limit our understanding to what is presented in hymns or popular caricatures. Otherwise, we may fail to gain an adequate understanding of heaven.

The Bible presents a new earth in which we live in our new bodies in the presence of God. The new earth is heaven as this is where God dwells. There will no longer be a separation between heaven and earth. This is where those in Christ will live for all eternity, so let's treasure what the Bible reveals to us.

God's plan of redemption for his creation and his people is complete. The establishment of the new heavens and new earth is the final aspect of the return of Christ. The second coming of Christ does not establish a kingdom on this present earth for one thousand years but instead consummates the current spiritual kingdom in the new heavens and new earth for all eternity.

Revealed in the Old Testament

Naturally, the Old Testament is the first place where the new heavens and new earth are revealed. Let's begin with Isaiah's description:

"For behold, I create new heavens
and a new earth,
and the former things shall not be remembered
or come into mind.
But be glad and rejoice forever
in that which I create;
for behold, I create Jerusalem to be a joy,
and her people to be a gladness.
I will rejoice in Jerusalem
and be glad in my people;
no more shall be heard in it the sound of weeping
and the cry of distress.
No more shall there be in it
an infant who lives but a few days,
or an old man who does not fill out his days,
for the young man shall die a hundred years old,
and the sinner a hundred years old shall be accursed.
They shall build houses and inhabit them;
they shall plant vineyards and eat their fruit.
They shall not build and another inhabit;
they shall not plant and another eat;
for like the days of a tree shall the days of my people be,
and my chosen shall long enjoy the work of their hands.
They shall not labor in vain
or bear children for calamity,
for they shall be the offspring of the blessed of the LORD,
and their descendants with them.
Before they call I will answer;
while they are yet speaking I will hear.
The wolf and the lamb shall graze together;
the lion shall eat straw like the ox,
and dust shall be the serpent's food.
They shall not hurt or destroy
in all my holy mountain,"
says the LORD. (Isaiah 65:17–25)

This is a beautiful passage—but also a difficult one. Dispensationalists claim this passage refers to the future millennium. There are several reasons, though, why this is incorrect. First, the Lord said through Isaiah, "For behold, I create new heavens and a new earth." This must refer to the new heavens and new earth described in Revelation 21, which is the final state for believers. Second, verse 18 tells us to "rejoice forever," not just for one thousand years. Third, verse 19 says, "No more shall be heard in it the sound of weeping and the cry of distress." This corresponds to Revelation 21:4:[91]

> He will wipe away every tear from their eyes, and death shall be no more,
> neither shall there be mourning, nor crying, nor pain anymore, for the
> former things have passed away.

There is a similar promise in Isaiah 25:8:

> He will swallow up death forever;
> and the Lord GOD will wipe away tears from all faces,
>   and the reproach of his people he will take away from all the earth,
>   for the LORD has spoken.

Admittedly, interpretive difficulties arise in Isaiah 65 with verse 20:

> No more shall there be in it
>   an infant who lives but a few days,
>   or an old man who does not fill out his days,
> for the young man shall die a hundred years old,
>   and the sinner a hundred years old shall be accursed.

How can death be mentioned if this passage refers to the final state? Dispensationalists claim this text refers to a future millennium, even though verse 17 just before it refers to new heavens and a new earth. What do we do with this? We should start by interpreting verse 20 within the context of the new heavens and new earth of verse 17. We've already seen in verse 19 that there will be no weeping in this heavenly Jerusalem. It is hard to imagine there still being death but no weeping. The first part of verse 20 says there will be

---

91   Hoekema, *The Bible and the Future*, 202.

no infant mortality, and older people will not die before finishing their life tasks. In other words, no one will die prematurely. People will live very long lives.

To understand the importance of this, we must remember two things. First, Isaiah is speaking to people under the Old Covenant. Long life was promised as a blessing for obedience in the Mosaic Covenant. For example, we see this in Deuteronomy 6:1–2:

> Now this is the commandment—the statutes and the rules—that the LORD your God commanded me to teach you, that you may do them in the land to which you are going over, to possess it, that you may fear the LORD your God, you and your son and your son's son, by keeping all his statutes and his commandments, which I command you, all the days of your life, and that your days may be long.

So, in the new heavens and new earth, people will live long lives, which were promised as a blessing of the Old Covenant.[92] The New Testament then expands that very long lifespan to last forever. The last part of Isaiah 65:22 supports this idea. It says, "For like the days of a tree shall the days of my people be, and my chosen shall long enjoy the work of their hands." Therefore, verse 20 does not say there will be people on the new earth that die.[93] *The Reformation Study Bible* says about verse 20,

> Premature death of infants or persons in midcareer can provoke the thought that life is meaningless. Such early death, as also the transfer of one person's reward to another person who has not earned it (v. 22), is part of God's judgment on sin. God promises to remove this curse from His people .... This is possible because Christ has come and fulfilled the terms of the Law, meriting its blessings for Himself and all those who are in Him.[94]

On the new earth, we will experience only the blessings earned by Christ. So, Isaiah 65:17–25 must refer only to the new heavens and new earth. Assigning it to a future millennium creates more problems than it solves. Remember, we must interpret the unclear in light of the clear. Given the Bible does not teach there will be a future one-thousand-year period, Isaiah 65:17–25 cannot refer to a future millennium.

---

92   Dean Davis, *The High King of Heaven* (Enumclaw, WA: Redemption Press, 2014), 214.
93   Hoekema, *The Bible and the Future*, 203.
94   Study note on Isaiah 65:20, in *The Reformation Study Bible* (Sanford, FL: Reformation Trust Publishing, 2015), 1247.

The second thing to remember that helps us understand Isaiah 65:20 is we are living in the "already" and "not yet." The new creation began with the resurrection of Christ, but we don't yet see the fullness of the new creation. Isaiah 65:25 says,

> The wolf and the lamb shall graze together;
> the lion shall eat straw like the ox,
> and dust shall be the serpent's food.
> They shall not hurt or destroy
> in all my holy mountain.

In the new heavens and new earth, there will be no hurt or destruction in a very specific place: "in all my holy mountain." Those who want to apply this to a future millennium say the conditions described in Isaiah 65:25 must apply worldwide on the current earth. However, the context is God's holy mountain. Isaiah 65:18–19 refer to Jerusalem, and God's holy mountain is Mount Zion in Jerusalem. What does the New Testament say about the holy mountain? Look at Hebrews 12:18–24:

> For you have not come to what may be touched, a blazing fire and darkness and gloom and a tempest and the sound of a trumpet and a voice whose words made the hearers beg that no further messages be spoken to them. For they could not endure the order that was given, "If even a beast touches the mountain, it shall be stoned." Indeed, so terrifying was the sight that Moses said, "I tremble with fear." But you have come to Mount Zion and to the city of the living God, the heavenly Jerusalem, and to innumerable angels in festal gathering, and to the assembly of the firstborn who are enrolled in heaven, and to God, the judge of all, and to the spirits of the righteous made perfect, and to Jesus, the mediator of a new covenant, and to the sprinkled blood that speaks a better word than the blood of Abel.

We *have come* to Mount Zion and to the city of the living God. We *have come* to the heavenly Jerusalem by the Holy Spirit. What we will have in fullness on the new earth is now ours in the Holy Spirit. Also, we are part of the assembly of the firstborn who are enrolled in heaven. The Greek word for assembly is *ekklesia*, which is also translated as *church*. On the new earth, we will experience the fullness of what we now have through the Holy Spirit. As Paul says in 1 Corinthians 2:9–10,

But, as it is written,

"What no eye has seen, nor ear heard,
nor the heart of man imagined,
what God has prepared for those who love him"—

these things God has revealed to us through the Spirit. For the Spirit searches everything, even the depths of God.

Paul quotes Isaiah 64:4 to show no one knows or can even imagine what God has prepared for those who love him. But he goes on to say that God has revealed through the Spirit those things we can't know or imagine. These things revealed by the Spirit have been written in the Word of God, and the Spirit gives us understanding of these things. Paul does not mean God has revealed everything, but God has given us a taste of eternity now, through the Word and the Spirit. The point is that we see now partially in the Church what the new earth will be like in its fullness.

Similar wording is found in Isaiah 11:6–9:

The wolf shall dwell with the lamb,
and the leopard shall lie down with the young goat,
and the calf and the lion and the fattened calf together;
and a little child shall lead them.
The cow and the bear shall graze;
their young shall lie down together;
and the lion shall eat straw like the ox.
The nursing child shall play over the hole of the cobra,
and the weaned child shall put his hand on the adder's den.
They shall not hurt or destroy
in all my holy mountain;
for the earth shall be full of the knowledge of the LORD
as the waters cover the sea.

These verses also proclaim that on God's holy mountain peace will occur between natural enemies. However, if we limit the meaning to "Animals will be nice to each other and to us on the new earth," then we have missed the point. The Lord is saying the enmity brought about by the Fall will be gone. We should experience this now in the Church through the Holy Spirit. Where can Jews and Arabs dwell together peacefully? Where can black and white love one another? This should happen in the Church. Unity is limited now due to the weakness of the flesh, but in our final home, there will be no separation or animosity among God's people. As verse 9 says, "The earth shall be full of the knowledge of the LORD as the waters cover the sea."[95]

Finally, let's briefly consider Ezekiel 40–48. (I will discuss these chapters in more depth later in the chapter on Ezekiel's temple.[96]) As a preview, one of the main points of that chapter is Ezekiel's temple will not be physically built in Jerusalem during a future millennium. The picture given by Ezekiel actually points us to the new heavens and new earth.

In chapter 47 Ezekiel described the water coming from the temple, and the water eventually becomes a river no one can cross. There are fruit trees on each side of the river continually producing fruit for the healing of the nations. He then gives the division of the land and describes the city. Similar descriptions are given in chapters 21 and 22 of Revelation concerning the new Jerusalem.[97] Consider Ezekiel 48:35, the last verse of the book:

> The circumference of the city shall be 18,000 cubits. And the name of the city from that time on shall be, The LORD Is There.

Revealed in the New Testament

The Old Testament presents the new heavens and new earth as the place where God will dwell forever with his people. The New Testament gives us a few more details.

Let's begin with 2 Peter 3:10–13:

> But the day of the Lord will come like a thief, and then the heavens will pass away with a roar, and the heavenly bodies will be burned up and dissolved, and the earth and the works that are done on it will be exposed. Since all these things are thus to be dissolved, what sort of people ought you to be in lives of holiness and godliness, waiting for and hastening the coming of the day of God, because of which the heavens will be set on fire and dissolved, and the heavenly bodies will melt as they burn! But according to his promise we are waiting for new heavens and a new earth in which righteousness dwells.

Peter assures us of God's coming judgment. As a part of that judgment, the present universe and the earth will be burned and dissolved in order to remove all sin. We are to

---

95 Hoekema, *The Bible and the Future*, 203.
96 See chapter 14, "Ezekiel's Temple."
97 Hoekema, *The Bible and the Future*, 205.

expect new heavens and a new earth marked by righteousness. This raises the question of whether the burning and dissolving taught by Peter means the current physical universe will be annihilated, and God will start over, or if Peter means the current physical universe will be refined and renewed. Peter's language sounds like annihilation, but the rest of Scripture does not allow that interpretation.[98] The creation is not looking forward to annihilation, but renewal. Also, Acts 3:19–21 refers to "the time for restoring all things." So, the new heavens and new earth will be the present creation, but free of all corruption.

The most extended and beautiful description of the new heavens and new earth is found in Revelation 21 and 22. I will briefly make some observations beginning with Revelation 21:1–4:

> Then I saw a new heaven and a new earth, for the first heaven and the first earth had passed away, and the sea was no more. And I saw the holy city, new Jerusalem, coming down out of heaven from God, prepared as a bride adorned for her husband. And I heard a loud voice from the throne saying, "Behold, the dwelling place of God is with man. He will dwell with them, and they will be his people, and God himself will be with them as their God. He will wipe away every tear from their eyes, and death shall be no more, neither shall there be mourning, nor crying, nor pain anymore, for the former things have passed away."

The "holy city" is adorned as a bride, which should clue us in as to what this city represents. Some expect a literal city that has been orbiting the earth to descend, but that interpretation misses the picture given by John. Verses 9 and 10 give us the clear identification of the city:

> Then came one of the seven angels who had the seven bowls full of the seven last plagues and spoke to me, saying, "Come, I will show you the Bride, the wife of the Lamb." And he carried me away in the Spirit to a great, high mountain, and showed me the holy city Jerusalem coming down out of heaven from God.

An angel tells John about the bride, the wife of the Lamb. The bride of Christ is the Church. Jesus is presented as the bridegroom, and the Church is his bride (Ephesians 5:25–27; Revelation 19:9–11). What does John see? He sees the holy city Jerusalem

---

98   See Hoekema, *The Bible and the Future*, 280–81 for a more thorough explanation.

coming down out of heaven. As Paul said in Galatians 4:26, "The Jerusalem above is free, and she is our mother." In the past, God dwelled in Jerusalem through the earthly temple, but in this holy city, he dwells in fullness. Ezekiel said the name of the city is "The LORD is There" (Ezekiel 48:35). Because God dwells on the new earth with his people, there will literally be heaven on earth. There will be no distinction between what we think of as heaven and life on the new earth. Believers will be in heaven and on earth at the same time. This is the ultimate fulfillment of God's promise in Ezekiel 37:27:

> My dwelling place shall be with them, and I will be their God, and they shall be my people.

This promise is found throughout Scripture:

> I will dwell among the people of Israel and will be their God. (Exodus 29:45)

> For this is the covenant that I will make with the house of Israel after those days, declares the LORD: I will put my law within them, and I will write it on their hearts. And I will be their God, and they shall be my people. (Jeremiah 31:33)

> While the man was standing beside me, I heard one speaking to me out of the temple, and he said to me, "Son of man, this is the place of my throne and the place of the soles of my feet, where I will dwell in the midst of the people of Israel forever. (Ezekiel 43:6–7)

> Sing and rejoice, O daughter of Zion, for behold, I come and I will dwell in your midst, declares the LORD. And many nations shall join themselves to the LORD in that day, and shall be my people. And I will dwell in your midst, and you shall know that the LORD of hosts has sent me to you. (Zechariah 2:10–11)

> What agreement has the temple of God with idols? For we are the temple of the living God; as God said,
> "I will make my dwelling among them and walk among them, and I will be their God, and they shall be my people." (2 Corinthians 6:16)

God can dwell there with his people because sin is no more.[99] That is why there will be no more death, mourning, crying, or pain.

Let's move on to Revelation 21:9–14:

> Then came one of the seven angels who had the seven bowls full of the seven last plagues and spoke to me, saying, "Come, I will show you the Bride, the wife of the Lamb." And he carried me away in the Spirit to a great, high mountain, and showed me the holy city Jerusalem coming down out of heaven from God, having the glory of God, its radiance like a most rare jewel, like a jasper, clear as crystal. It had a great, high wall, with twelve gates, and at the gates twelve angels, and on the gates the names of the twelve tribes of the sons of Israel were inscribed—on the east three gates, on the north three gates, on the south three gates, and on the west three gates. And the wall of the city had twelve foundations, and on them were the twelve names of the twelve apostles of the Lamb.

The city gates have the names of the twelve tribes of Israel, as was prophesied in chapter 48 of Ezekiel. There are also twelve foundations with the names of the apostles. Ephesians 2:19–22 uses the same imagery to describe the Church. The Church is built on the foundation of the apostles and prophets:

> So then you are no longer strangers and aliens, but you are fellow citizens with the saints and members of the household of God, built on the foundation of the apostles and prophets, Christ Jesus himself being the cornerstone, in whom the whole structure, being joined together, grows into a holy temple in the Lord. In him you also are being built together into a dwelling place for God by the Spirit.

In Revelation, the city and the temple are the same. Also, notice the unity of the Old and New Testament believers with the gates named after the twelve tribes and the foundations named after the twelve apostles.

Now, look at Revelation 21:15–21:

---

99   Hoekema, *The Bible and the Future*, 285.

> And the one who spoke with me had a measuring rod of gold to measure the city and its gates and walls. The city lies foursquare, its length the same as its width. And he measured the city with his rod, 12,000 stadia. Its length and width and height are equal. He also measured its wall, 144 cubits by human measurement, which is also an angel's measurement. The wall was built of jasper, while the city was pure gold, like clear glass. The foundations of the wall of the city were adorned with every kind of jewel. The first was jasper, the second sapphire, the third agate, the fourth emerald, the fifth onyx, the sixth carnelian, the seventh chrysolite, the eighth beryl, the ninth topaz, the tenth chrysoprase, the eleventh jacinth, the twelfth amethyst. And the twelve gates were twelve pearls, each of the gates made of a single pearl, and the street of the city was pure gold, like transparent glass.

The angel speaking to John measures the city. The measurement is 12,000 stadia. Please don't think of this as a literal measurement. The number is merely giving us a picture. The number twelve represents God working in the world. He worked through the twelve tribes in the Old Testament and the twelve apostles in the New Testament. That number is multiplied by ten cubed to signify completeness. What is most important, though, is the length, width, and height are equal. This means the city is a cube. Again, don't focus on the shape but rather on what that shape tells us. What is the only other cube in the Bible? First Kings 6:20 tells us the inner sanctuary of the temple, the Holy of Holies, was twenty cubits long, twenty cubits wide, and twenty cubits high—a cube. The New Jerusalem is the new Holy of Holies. The wall is 144 cubits, which is twelve times twelve. John then gives a description of the foundations inlaid with various precious stones, the gates made of pearl, and the streets made of gold. Whether our dwelling place with God has literal streets of gold or literal gates of pearl is not important. These descriptions are intended to give us a taste of how pure and perfect the city will be.

Revelation 21:22–27 rounds out the chapter:

> And I saw no temple in the city, for its temple is the Lord God the Almighty and the Lamb. And the city has no need of sun or moon to shine on it, for the glory of God gives it light, and its lamp is the Lamb. By its light will the nations walk, and the kings of the earth will bring their glory into it, and its gates will never be shut by day—and there will be no night there. They will bring into it the glory and the honor of the nations. But nothing

unclean will ever enter it, nor anyone who does what is detestable or false, but only those who are written in the Lamb's book of life.

There is no temple because the Lord Himself dwells there. Light comes from the glory of God and from the Lamb. Compare the reference to the nations in verse 24 to Isaiah 60:1–3:

> Arise, shine, for your light has come,
>   and the glory of the LORD has risen upon you.
> For behold, darkness shall cover the earth,
>   and thick darkness the peoples;
> but the LORD will arise upon you,
>   and his glory will be seen upon you.
> And nations shall come to your light,
>   and kings to the brightness of your rising.

The gates of the city will never be shut because it will never be night. Cities would close their gates at night to protect the citizens from invaders coming in the night, but there are no more enemies to menace God's people, so that is not necessary here. There will never be another Satan creeping into God's garden. No more threats exist. Instead of evil entering the gates, a multitude from every nation, tribe, people, and language will enter (Revelation 5:9; 7:9). All those invited to the wedding feast will enter through the gates. All those whose names are written in the Lamb's book of life will be there.

Finally, look at Revelation 22:1–5:

> Then the angel showed me the river of the water of life, bright as crystal, flowing from the throne of God and of the Lamb through the middle of the street of the city; also, on either side of the river, the tree of life with its twelve kinds of fruit, yielding its fruit each month. The leaves of the tree were for the healing of the nations. No longer will there be anything accursed, but the throne of God and of the Lamb will be in it, and his servants will worship him. They will see his face, and his name will be on their foreheads. And night will be no more. They will need no light of lamp or sun, for the Lord God will be their light, and they will reign forever and ever.

Here, we find the same description of the river and the trees that are in Ezekiel. This is where God dwells with his people. Instead of giving us the name of the city "The LORD is There" as in Ezekiel 48:35, John shows us why he named the city, "The LORD is There." The throne of God and the Lamb will be there. We will see his face, and his name will be on our foreheads. The Lord himself will be our light, and there will be no night. The one who came as the light of the world to rescue those in darkness will be our light for eternity.

The Regeneration

Jesus spoke of the new heavens and new earth. He predicts the new heavens and new earth in Matthew 19:28 where he refers to "the regeneration":

> Jesus said to them, "Truly, I say to you, in the new world, when the Son of Man will sit on his glorious throne, you who have followed me will also sit on twelve thrones, judging the twelve tribes of Israel.

The ESV has "in the new world," but the footnote shows the direct translation of the Greek, which is "in the regeneration." The NASB has "in the regeneration" with the footnote "Or renewal; i.e., the new world." The CSB and NIV say, "the renewal of all things."

Dispensationalists claim that in this passage, Jesus is referring to the future millennium, but the language and the context rule that out.[100] Jesus is not referring to a future millennium but the final state in the New Jerusalem. The only other place where the Greek word translated as "regeneration" is used is Titus 3:5:

> He saved us, not because of works done by us in righteousness, but according to his own mercy, by the washing of regeneration and renewal of the Holy Spirit.

---

100 Dispensationalists understand the regeneration (or renewal) to refer to conditions during the millennium for multiple reasons but primarily due to their commitment to a Church–Israel distinction. For dispensationalists, this is reinforced by Jesus telling the disciples "you who have followed me will also sit on twelve thrones, judging the twelve tribes of Israel." However, the rest of the New Testament does not allow for that ongoing distinction. The disciples understood Jesus to be saying that they would be judging the whole people of God. At this point, the concept of the people of God including the Gentiles was lost on them.

In Titus regeneration refers to our spiritual regeneration, which is being brought from death to life. Those saved by Christ are transferred from the realm of death to the realm of life. So also, the new world (the regeneration) is the old world renewed, so there is no more sin, no more corruption, no more death. Not only does this not describe the dispensational understanding of the millennium, but it also does not describe the historic premillennial understanding of the millennium or the postmillennial understanding of the millennium.

Furthermore, we read in Matthew 19:29,

> And everyone who has left houses or brothers or sisters or father or mother or children or lands, for my name's sake, will receive a hundred-fold and will inherit eternal life.

In the regeneration (the new world), rewards will be enjoyed, with the ultimate reward being eternal life. Eternal life is not simply life unending but true knowledge of and fellowship with the true God and with Jesus. Jesus defines eternal life in John 17:3:

> And this is eternal life, that they know you, the only true God, and Jesus Christ whom you have sent.

In the final state, we will see Jesus face to face (1 Corinthians 13:12). We will see him as he is (1 John 3:2) because we will be with him.

Summary

The Bible begins with God creating the heavens and earth. He then creates all living things with man as the crown of his creation. However, sin entered and corrupted man and creation. That's not the end of the story, though. The last Adam, the second man (1 Corinthians 15:45–49), has come and accomplished redemption on the cross. He rose from the grave demonstrating his victory over sin and death, and he now rules over all things. His return marks the fullness of his redemption and the undoing of the curse of sin. Redeemed mankind will dwell in sinless, incorruptible bodies on a restored, incorruptible earth in the presence of Christ himself. In our fallen flesh, we can't comprehend how glorious this will be, but in the new heavens and new earth, sin will no longer hinder us from pure praise to the Lord for all eternity.

Chapter 11

REDEMPTION COMPLETE

In the beginning, God created the heavens and the earth, and, in the end, God will create new heavens and new earth.

In the beginning, God created man and placed him in a garden with the tree of life and the tree of the knowledge of good and evil at the center. In the end, man will live in a city with a river running through its middle, and on either side of the river, there is the tree of life.

In the beginning, the first Adam sinned by eating the forbidden fruit of the tree of the knowledge of good and evil and plunged all mankind into sin and death. In the end, the last Adam (Jesus) will destroy all evil and death.

In the beginning, the first Adam was given authority over the earth by God, but the enemy usurped that authority through his temptation of Adam. In the end, the sinless last Adam will return all things to God. All that was undone in the fall of the first Adam is restored in Christ. When Jesus returns, redemption is complete—the redemption of his creation and the redemption of man. Christ's work as the last Adam will be fully consummated.

Redemption of Creation

We know from Genesis 3:17–19 and Romans 8:20–21 that Adam's sin brought corruption to the created realm. There is nothing living that doesn't die. Plants, trees, animals, fish, and humans all die. Civilizations rise and civilizations disappear. Everything that is made is temporary, wearing out like a garment (Isaiah 51:6). Nothing stays pristine. Buildings decay and roads crumble. However, the effects of sin will one day be gone from the created world. Let's consider again 2 Peter 3:10–13:

> But the day of the Lord will come like a thief, and then the heavens will pass away with a roar, and the heavenly bodies will be burned up and dissolved, and the earth and the works that are done on it will be exposed. Since all these things are thus to be dissolved, what sort of people ought you to be in lives of holiness and godliness, waiting for and hastening the coming of the day of God, because of which the heavens will be set on fire and dissolved, and the heavenly bodies will melt as they burn! But according to his promise we are waiting for new heavens and a new earth in which righteousness dwells.

This present creation is corrupted by sin, but when Jesus returns, the physical creation will be burned up and dissolved.[101] As Jesus said in Matthew 24:35, "Heaven and earth will pass away." Since all of creation was corrupted by the sin of Adam, all of creation must be renewed. Romans 8:19 links our full redemption and the redemption of creation:

> For the creation waits with eager longing for the revealing of the sons of God.

The "revealing of the sons of God" occurs when Jesus returns, and "creation waits with eager longing" for that day.

Redemption of Man

However, the redemption of creation is not possible without the redemption of man. Without the incarnation and the life, death, resurrection, and ascension of Jesus, there is no restoration of creation. Colossians 1:18–20 says of Jesus,

> And he is the head of the body, the church. He is the beginning, the firstborn from the dead, that in everything he might be preeminent. For in him all the fullness of God was pleased to dwell, and through him to reconcile to himself all things, whether on earth or in heaven, making peace by the blood of his cross.

---

101 This does not refer to the annihilation of the creation, but a cleansing and restoration of the creation. The new heavens and new earth are the current heavens and earth renewed. See chapter 10, "The New Heavens and New Earth."

The blood Jesus shed on the cross reconciles all things to God. The scope of "all things" is "on earth or in heaven." Thus, when Christ redeemed man on the cross, his redeeming work applied to every person for whom Christ died and every place affected by evil. Jesus's resurrection gave him firstborn from the dead status, which means his resurrection is the preeminent resurrection. There is no reconciliation or redemption apart from his resurrection.

However, Christ's resurrection is not only the preeminent (firstborn) resurrection but also the firstfruits resurrection. Let's look at 1 Corinthians 15:20–28:

> But in fact Christ has been raised from the dead, the firstfruits of those who have fallen asleep. For as by a man came death, by a man has come also the resurrection of the dead. For as in Adam all die, so also in Christ shall all be made alive. But each in his own order: Christ the firstfruits, then at his coming those who belong to Christ. Then comes the end, when he delivers the kingdom to God the Father after destroying every rule and every authority and power. For he must reign until he has put all his enemies under his feet. The last enemy to be destroyed is death. For "God has put all things in subjection under his feet." But when it says, "all things are put in subjection," it is plain that he is excepted who put all things in subjection under him. When all things are subjected to him, then the Son himself will also be subjected to him who put all things in subjection under him, that God may be all in all.

Verses 20–23 contrast the man Adam with the man Christ. All who are in Adam die because Adam sinned and brought forth death. All who are in Christ live because Christ defeated death as a man. Christ's resurrection is the firstfruit that guarantees the resurrection of the dead in Christ.

In the Old Testament, the firstfruits of a crop were given to the Lord and were representative of the remainder of the harvest. The firstfruits of the crop proved there would be a harvest to come. So, because Christ rose from the dead (the firstfruits), those in Christ are guaranteed to rise from the dead when he returns. This is the hope of those who are found in Christ at his second coming.

On the other hand, Paul also describes the end of all opposed to Christ:

> Then comes the end, when he delivers the kingdom to God the Father after destroying every rule and every authority and power. (1 Corinthians 15:24)

Paul is speaking of the completion of the redemptive work of Christ. When those in Christ have been raised (v. 23) and "every rule and every authority and power" are no more, Christ hands over the completed kingdom to God the Father. This happens once Jesus has cast Satan (Revelation 20:10), Death and Hades (Revelation 20:14), all unbelievers (Revelation 20:15), and the corrupt world system along with all false worship (Revelation 19:20) into the lake of fire.

Note the flow from verse 25 through the first part of verse 27:

- For he must reign until he has put all his enemies under his feet. (v. 25)
  - The last enemy to be destroyed is death. (v. 26)
- For "God has put all things in subjection under his feet." (v. 27a)

The destruction of death is surrounded by the supremacy of Christ as represented by the phrase "under his feet." Notice Jesus *must* reign (v. 25), not just *will* reign, until all enemies are under his feet, and God *has* put all things under the feet of Jesus.[102] According to 1 Peter 3:22, at Christ's ascension, angels, authorities, and powers were *subjected* to him. Everything and everyone is under the authority of Jesus, but there is coming a day when all angels, authorities, and powers opposed to God will be *destroyed* by him (Revelation 19:17–21; 20:7–10). The last enemy is death, and Jesus conquered death through his own death and resurrection. He will abolish death at his return (1 Corinthians 15:26; Revelation 20:14).

We see that 1 Corinthians 15:27–28 shows that all Christ has done and will do is for the glory of the Father. The Father subjected all things to Jesus, but the Father was not subjected to Jesus (v. 27). In other words, in Jesus's role as redeemer and mediator, he is under the authority of the Father. The Son as the second person of the Trinity is not in submission to the Father, but the Word that became flesh (John 1:14) is submitted to the Father.[103]

The first phrase of verse 28 says, "When all things are subjected to him [Jesus]." That phrase refers to the completion of Jesus's work as the last Adam, which Paul explained in verses 24–27. The next phrase of verse 28 says, "Then the Son himself will also be subjected to him who put all things in subjection under him." Paul is not saying Jesus is not currently submitted to the Father. Paul is proclaiming that once Christ's work is complete as the God-man, he will remain submitted to the Father so "that God may be all in all." In other words, God the Father will receive all the glory. Paul addresses this in Philippians 2:8–11:

---

102 Paul is quoting Psalm 8:6 in verse 27. See also Matthew 11:27; 28:19; and Ephesians 1:22.
103 See John 8:28; 14:10, 31.

And being found in human form, he [Jesus] humbled himself by becoming obedient to the point of death, even death on a cross. Therefore God has highly exalted him and bestowed on him the name that is above every name, so that at the name of Jesus every knee should bow, in heaven and on earth and under the earth, and every tongue confess that Jesus Christ is Lord, to the glory of God the Father.

Every tongue eventually confesses Jesus Christ is Lord, and this is done to *the glory of God the Father*. "That God may be all in all" is another way of saying all glory goes to God the Father. Simon Kistemaker says,

Christ's mediatorial work comes to an end when he hands over the kingdom to God the Father. When his people eventually rise from the dead and are glorified, he no longer is their mediator, for his redemptive task is finished. Sin will be blotted out, Satan with his hordes powerless and consigned to hell, and death destroyed. Then Christ, who with his glorified body brought earth to heaven, will bring heaven to earth at the renewal of all things.[104]

The Father gave everything to the Son, through whom he created all things (John 1:3; Hebrews 1:2) and through whom salvation was accomplished (John 14:6; Acts 4:12). Therefore, once his work is finished, Jesus (the Son incarnate) hands all things back to the Father. At that point, the redemptive and mediatorial work of Jesus will be complete. The last act of Christ as our redeemer is to hand over the kingdom to the Father, so God is all in all.

Summary

Christ restores what Adam lost. The restoration began with his incarnation when Jesus defeated sin and death. As 1 Corinthians 15:56 says, "The sting of death is sin, and the power of sin is the law." In other words, the result of sin is death, and the law reveals sin. Sin had no power over Christ because he delighted in and fulfilled God's law. Death had no power over Christ because his perfect sacrifice propitiated (satisfied) God's wrath against sin. Christ's resurrection from the dead demonstrated the sufficiency of his sacrifice. It was not possible for him to be held by death (Acts 2:24).

---

104 Simon J. Kistemaker, *Exposition of the First Epistle to the Corinthians*, New Testament Commentary (Grand Rapids, MI: Baker Books, 1993), 557.

Amillennialism presents the return of Christ as an all-encompassing event in which this victory of Christ over sin, death, and the grave is realized in full. Those in Christ are raised to live with him forever in the New Jerusalem.[105] All those not in Christ, along with Satan and all evil, are cast into the lake of fire.[106]

The day Jesus returns will be a glorious day. May we always long for the day when we are with the great multitude crying out, "Hallelujah! Salvation and glory and power belong to our God" (Revelation 19:1).

---

105 Matthew 25:34–40; 1 Thessalonians 4:13–17; 1 Corinthians 15:50–56; Revelation 7:9–17; 11:15–18; 19:6–8; 21:1–22:5
106 Matthew 25:41–46; 2 Thessalonians 1:5–10; Revelation 6:12–17; 11:18–19; 14:14–20; 16:17–21; 19:17–21; 20:11–15

PART 3:

AMILLENNIAL INTERPRETATION

The Church has various understandings of the Olivet Discourse in Matthew 24–25, the seventy weeks in Daniel 9, and Ezekiel's temple in Ezekiel 40–48. Chapters 12–14 consider these passages from an amillennial perspective.

Chapter 12

THE OLIVET DISCOURSE

Matthew 24–25 is called the Olivet Discourse because Jesus gave the discourse on the Mount of Olives. In this chapter, I will focus on Matthew 24 and its parallels in Mark 13 and Luke 21. My goal is not to give a full exposition but rather to provide an overall sense of the chapter because of the importance of the Olivet Discourse to eschatology.

In his book *A Case for Amillennialism*, Kim Riddlebarger gives three basic interpretive schemes for the Olivet Discourse. The first is the preterist view, which sees the events predicted by Jesus in Matthew 24 as having been fulfilled in the destruction of Jerusalem in AD 70. Even the passages that seem to clearly speak of Jesus returning in a glorious manner are understood as referring to God's judgment on Israel when the Romans destroyed Jerusalem. To the full preterists, the end of the age is the end of the Jewish age—a view that lands outside of orthodox Christian doctrine. On the other hand, partial preterism is considered within orthodoxy because its adherents maintain the expectation of Christ's future return.

The second interpretive scheme is futurism. In this scheme, even though there is some reference to the destruction of Jerusalem, the bulk of the prophecy in Matthew 24 looks forward to the return of Christ. Dispensationalists believe this prophecy also refers to a rebuilt temple in the restored nation of Israel, and they point to the establishment of the present-day nation of Israel in 1948 as a fulfillment of prophecy. In their view, the restored nation of Israel will suffer great tribulation at the hand of the Antichrist after the secret rapture of the church.

The third interpretive scheme focuses on the questions the disciples asked Jesus. Jesus prophesied the destruction of the temple and his return at the end of the age. The events surrounding the destruction of the temple foreshadowed the events surrounding his return. Therefore, this passage does not exclusively apply to the future, nor was the passage completely fulfilled by the events of AD 70.[107]

Setting

Let's set the context for the Olivet Discourse. Jesus spoke these words during his last week in Jerusalem before his death. After the triumphal entry into Jerusalem at the beginning of Matthew 21, Jesus cleanses the temple and gives several parables of judgment on the Jews. These include the parable of the two sons, the parable of the tenants, and the parable of the wedding feast. Some of the Pharisees follow up by asking Jesus about paying taxes to Caesar. Similarly, some Sadducees ask Jesus about the resurrection. A lawyer then asks Jesus about the great commandment, and Jesus asks questions of his own to the Pharisees, "What do you think about the Christ? Whose son is he?" (Matthew 22:42). In the next chapter Jesus declares seven woes against the scribes and the Pharisees. He then concludes with his lament over Jerusalem in Matthew 23:37–39:

> O Jerusalem, Jerusalem, the city that kills the prophets and stones those who are sent to it! How often would I have gathered your children together as a hen gathers her brood under her wings, and you were not willing! See, your house is left to you desolate. For I tell you, you will not see me again, until you say, "Blessed is he who comes in the name of the Lord."

In Mark and Luke, the story of the widow who gave her two small coins at the temple precedes the Gospel writers' versions of the discourse. In all three accounts, there is mention of the magnificence of the temple, followed by Jesus saying it will be destroyed. Matthew 24:1–2 puts it this way,

> Jesus left the temple and was going away, when his disciples came to point out to him the buildings of the temple. But he answered them, "You see all these, do you not? Truly, I say to you, there will not be left here one stone upon another that will not be thrown down."

---

107 Riddlebarger, *A Case for Amillennialism*, 189.

The lament of Jesus in Luke's Gospel includes a prediction of the destruction of Jerusalem in which Jesus said not one stone will be left upon another stone:

> And when he drew near and saw the city, he wept over it, saying, "Would that you, even you, had known on this day the things that make for peace! But now they are hidden from your eyes. For the days will come upon you, when your enemies will set up a barricade around you and surround you and hem you in on every side and tear you down to the ground, you and your children within you. And they will not leave one stone upon another in you, because you did not know the time of your visitation." (Luke 19:41–44)

Jesus's prediction of the destruction of the temple at the beginning of the Olivet Discourse is the second time the disciples have heard Jesus prophesy its demise. The temple was the center of religious life and a source of pride for the Jews, so, at this point, they asked some questions.

The Questions

When the disciples have Jesus alone, they ask him about his prediction. Matthew 24:3 says, "As he sat on the Mount of Olives, the disciples came to him privately, saying, 'Tell us, when will these things be, and what will be the sign of your coming and of the end of the age?'" Notice that the disciples asked two questions. The first question is "When will these things be?" The second question is "What will be the sign of your coming and of the end of the age?"

The key to interpreting this passage is understanding the disciples' questions. Clearly, the disciples linked the destruction of the temple with the end of the age. They did not comprehend life without a physical temple. Also, note their second question shows they believed the return of Christ and the end of the age were tied together. So, when Jesus answers their questions, he does so by speaking of two judgments: a judgment that would come on Jerusalem within a generation and a final judgment at the end of the age.

The interpretive difficulty comes in determining which judgment is in view. What we will see is there is some intermingling of the two judgments, with the judgment on Jerusalem in some ways foreshadowing the final judgment.[108] Given that, let me propose that

---

108 Riddlebarger, *A Case for Amillennialism*, 191.

we divide the chapter into two sections. Verses 4–35 deal primarily with the judgment of Jerusalem, and verses 36–44 deal primarily with the final judgment. Verse 35 indicates the end of the prophecy about the destruction of Jerusalem because of what Jesus said in verses 34 and 35,

> Truly, I say to you, this generation will not pass away until all these things take place. Heaven and earth will pass away, but my words will not pass away.

Jesus said what he is prophesying about Jerusalem will be accomplished within a generation, and we can be sure of it because his words do not fail.

On a side note, dispensationalists see this as referring to the generation that sees the restoration of Israel. That's why so many were expecting the rapture within a generation of the establishment of the present state of Israel (1948). Clearly, that was in error, as we are well past that point. Jesus was not referring to a future generation but rather to the generation who was alive when he gave the prophecy. The prophecy concerning his return begins in verse 36:

> But concerning that day and hour no one knows, not even the angels of heaven, nor the Son, but the Father only. For as were the days of Noah, so will be the coming of the Son of Man. (Matthew 24:36–37)

We will deal with this more later, but, when Jesus said, "that day," the disciples would have understood Jesus to be referring to the day of the Lord—the Day of Judgment.

Judgment on Jerusalem

We are going to linger on Matthew 24:4–14 since this first section of the chapter is the most disputed:

> And Jesus answered them, "See that no one leads you astray. For many will come in my name, saying, 'I am the Christ,' and they will lead many astray. And you will hear of wars and rumors of wars. See that you are not alarmed, for this must take place, but the end is not yet. For nation will rise against nation, and kingdom against kingdom, and there will be famines and earthquakes in various places. All these are but the beginning of the birth pains. Then they will deliver you up to tribulation and put you to

death, and you will be hated by all nations for my name's sake. And then many will fall away and betray one another and hate one another. And many false prophets will arise and lead many astray. And because lawlessness will be increased, the love of many will grow cold. But the one who endures to the end will be saved. And this gospel of the kingdom will be proclaimed throughout the whole world as a testimony to all nations, and then the end will come."

It would be a mistake to assign what Christ said in these verses solely to the future. Jesus is giving a warning to the generation of his twelve disciples. Notice Jesus starts by warning them not to be deceived. Just as the Bible proclaims there will be deceivers throughout the gospel age, Jesus tells the disciples that deceivers will show up right away. There were many self-appointed "messiahs" before the destruction of Jerusalem. For example, Josephus tells of an insurrectionist who preached to an armed multitude at Mount Gerizim. Josephus also tells of a man named Theudas, who called himself a prophet and promised to divide the Jordan River. He had many followers before the procurator of Judea executed him.

Acts 8 records the story of a magician, Simon Magus, who impressed many in Samaria. At another time, there was an Egyptian who came with thousands, and he promised that the walls of Jerusalem would fall at his command.[109] Josephus also reports of insurrectionists during the reigns of Claudius and Nero who claimed divine inspiration and empowerment for rebellion against Rome. In addition, there were plenty of wars and uprisings before Jerusalem's destruction.

In addition to false messiahs, there were also many famines and earthquakes in the first century. The historian Tacitus recorded major earthquakes in Antioch, Phrygia, and Laodicea before AD 70. There was a famine in the Roman Empire around AD 50. With this context in mind, remember what Jesus said in verse 8, "All these are but the beginning of the birth pains."

Jesus predicted betrayal, hatred, and persecution. We first think of the persecution of the Christians by Saul before he was Paul. The Jews martyred Stephen, and Herod ordered the beheading of James, the brother of John. Peter and Paul would experience persecution of their own, leading to their martyrdom. Nero executed many Christians after the great fire of Rome. The writings of Josephus confirm graphic details of the brutal conditions in Jerusalem before its fall. Jesus said that, because of this early persecution, "Many will turn

---

109 See Acts 21:38 where Paul is asked if he is the Egyptian who sparked a revolt.

from the faith," and "The love of most will grow cold."[110] This reminds us of the seed sown in the rocky soil from Matthew 13:20–21:

> As for what was sown on rocky ground, this is the one who hears the word and immediately receives it with joy, yet he has no root in himself, but endures for a while, and when tribulation or persecution arises on account of the word, immediately he falls away.

Those who endure to the end, those known by Jesus, will be saved.

If we see evidence of false messiahs, calamity, and persecution in the first century, what do we do with Matthew 24:14, which speaks of the gospel being preached to the whole world? I previously discussed this as a sign of the return of Christ.[111] What I didn't explain earlier are the conditions and events predicted by Jesus that have a double fulfillment. The gospel was preached in all the known world by AD 70, but, for us, this also applies to the return of Christ. We know the gospel will be preached to the whole world because Revelation 7:9 says there will be "a great multitude that no one could number, from every nation, from all tribes and peoples and languages, standing before the throne and before the Lamb."

Double Fulfillment

Let's pause to consider double fulfillment. Double fulfillment of prophecies is when there is a near-term fulfillment followed by a greater future fulfillment. We find this throughout the Bible. In 2 Samuel 7 God speaks through the prophet Nathan, telling David he will make David's name great and will build him a house. We then read in 2 Samuel 7:12–16,

> When your days are fulfilled and you lie down with your fathers, I will raise up your offspring after you, who shall come from your body, and I will establish his kingdom. He shall build a house for my name, and I will establish the throne of his kingdom forever. I will be to him a father, and he shall be to me a son. When he commits iniquity, I will discipline him with the rod of men, with the stripes of the sons of men, but my steadfast love will not depart from him, as I took it from Saul, whom I put away from

---

110 Daniel M. Doriani, *Matthew*, Reformed Expository Commentary (Phillipsburg, NJ: P&R, 2008), 2:353–56.

111 See chapter 4, "The Return of Christ."

before you. And your house and your kingdom shall be made sure forever before me. Your throne shall be established forever.

This prophecy applies initially to David's son, Solomon. When Solomon sinned, he was disciplined, but he was not removed from the throne as Saul was. However, Solomon's throne was not established forever—he died. There is clearly a further fulfillment, which we know points to Christ, the descendant of David who sits on the throne of David.

Another example of double fulfillment is the prophecy of Immanuel in Isaiah 7. The message was given first to King Ahaz, in the context of the threat of Assyrian invasion, and it was initially fulfilled in his time. However, the ultimate fulfillment of Isaiah 7 was revealed in the virgin birth of Jesus.[112] We see a similar double fulfillment of Jesus's words in Matthew 24. We will return to this shortly.

Abomination of Desolation

For now, though, let's move on to Matthew 24:15–28:

> So when you see the abomination of desolation spoken of by the prophet Daniel, standing in the holy place (let the reader understand), then let those who are in Judea flee to the mountains. Let the one who is on the housetop not go down to take what is in his house, and let the one who is in the field not turn back to take his cloak. And alas for women who are pregnant and for those who are nursing infants in those days! Pray that your flight may not be in winter or on a Sabbath. For then there will be great tribulation, such as has not been from the beginning of the world until now, no, and never will be. And if those days had not been cut short, no human being would be saved. But for the sake of the elect those days will be cut short. Then if anyone says to you, "Look, here is the Christ!" or "There he is!" do not believe it. For false christs and false prophets will arise and perform great signs and wonders, so as to lead astray, if possible, even the elect. See, I have told you beforehand. So, if they say to you, "Look, he is in the wilderness," do not go out. If they say, "Look, he is in the inner rooms," do not believe it. For as the lightning comes from the east and shines as far as the west, so will be the coming of the Son of Man. Wherever the corpse is, there the vultures will gather.

---

112 Doriani, *Matthew*, 351–52.

In this section of the Olivet Discourse, we immediately face the question, "What is the abomination of desolation?" Fortunately, Jesus tells us it comes from Daniel. In Daniel 7, Daniel has a dream of four beasts that represent four kings or kingdoms. The fourth beast has ten horns, but a "little horn" grows and displaces three of the horns. Daniel wants to know about this fourth beast, and he gets an explanation in Daniel 7:23–25:

> Thus he said: "As for the fourth beast,
> there shall be a fourth kingdom on earth,
>   which shall be different from all the kingdoms,
> and it shall devour the whole earth,
>   and trample it down, and break it to pieces.
> As for the ten horns, out of this kingdom ten kings shall arise,
>   and another shall arise after them;
> he shall be different from the former ones,
>   and shall put down three kings.
> He shall speak words against the Most High,
>   and shall wear out the saints of the Most High,
>   and shall think to change the times and the law;
> and they shall be given into his hand
>   for a time, times, and half a time."

Antiochus IV Epiphanes, a Hellenistic Syrian king, fulfilled this prophecy in 168 BC when he came against Jerusalem. (Note that the last part of his name, Epiphanes, is a title that means "God made manifest.") However, in Daniel 11, we see something similar. Daniel said of the king of the north, "And the king shall do as he wills. He shall exalt himself and magnify himself above every god, and shall speak astonishing things against the God of gods" (Daniel 11:36).

Daniel 7:25 and 11:36 were both fulfilled by Antiochus Epiphanes, who spoke "astonishing things" against "the Most High." Yet there appears to be another fulfillment. Twice Daniel speaks of the "abomination that makes desolate." In Daniel 11:31, again speaking of the king of the north, we read,

> Forces from him shall appear and profane the temple and fortress, and shall take away the regular burnt offering. And they shall set up the abomination that makes desolate.

Also, Daniel 12:11 says,

> And from the time that the regular burnt offering is taken away and the abomination that makes desolate is set up, there shall be 1,290 days.

Antiochus profaned the temple in Jerusalem by dedicating it to the Greek god Zeus. He ended the burnt offerings and substituted other pagan sacrifices including the sacrifice of pigs on the altar. The prophecies from Daniel were initially fulfilled by Antiochus IV Epiphanes in 168 BC, but based on this passage in Matthew, there would be another fulfillment to come. The near-term fulfillment of Matthew 24:15 was when the Roman army under Titus destroyed Jerusalem. Note the parallel passage in Luke 21:20:

> But when you see Jerusalem surrounded by armies, then know that its desolation has come near.

Whereas Matthew and Mark write, "when you see the abomination of desolation," Luke says, "when you see Jerusalem surrounded by armies." This is a reference to the Roman armies under Titus. The imperial armies carried idols and images for emperor worship. The temple would not only be desecrated, as it had been with Antiochus IV Epiphanes, but it would also be destroyed. Note that Jesus said that when the people see this, they are to flee. When the armies came, the Christians fled Jerusalem, but the Jews took shelter in Jerusalem. The Christian historian Eusebius, who lived from about AD 260 to AD 340, said this in his writings,

> On the other hand, the people of the Jerusalem church were commanded by an oracle given by revelation before the war to those in the city who were worthy of it to depart and dwell in one of the cities of Perea which they called Pella.[113]

There are those who doubt this account. The doubters say the Christians would have had to go through the Roman army to flee. Others, though, point out that the Roman armies led by Vespasian initially came to Jerusalem in AD 66 to stop the Jewish revolt against Roman rule. Because Nero died, Vespasian was recalled to Rome in AD 68 to

---

113 Eusebius, *Ecclesiastical History*, book III, v. 3, quoted in William Hendriksen, *The Gospel of Matthew*, New Testament Commentary (Grand Rapids, MI: Baker Book House, 1973), 858.

become emperor. When the armies left, the Christians fled, but the Jews remained, as they thought the threat from Rome was over. However, Titus, the son of Vespasian, returned and destroyed Jerusalem. By then, most Christians were already gone. The words of Jesus, though, give the sense that as soon as you hear about armies coming or see them on the horizon, get out. Do go back for anything. Just leave. This shows Jesus was speaking of the destruction of Jerusalem.

Great Tribulation

After he gave the warning to flee, Jesus said there would be great tribulation. This tribulation not only refers to the tribulation at the time of the destruction of Jerusalem, but it also points to a future period of tribulation.[114] There were unspeakable horrors endured during the siege of Jerusalem, such as severe famine and infant cannibalism. Look again at Matthew 24:21–22:

> For then there will be great tribulation, such as has not been from the beginning of the world until now, no, and never will be. And if those days had not been cut short, no human being would be saved. But for the sake of the elect those days will be cut short.

Because Jesus said there will never be another tribulation like this one, a future tribulation is indicated. There has been much pagan and Christian suffering since AD 70 that surpasses what happened during the siege of Jerusalem. Just as God cut short the tribulation during the destruction of Jerusalem for the sake of the Christians, he will cut short the persecution of his people at the end. This is double fulfillment.

After this, Jesus again warns about false christs. This was not only a warning to the generation that experienced the destruction of Jerusalem, but it also shows the destruction of Jerusalem was not the end of the age. Note what Jesus said in Matthew 24:23-28:

> Then if anyone says to you, "Look, here is the Christ!" or "There he is!" do not believe it. For false christs and false prophets will arise and perform great signs and wonders, so as to lead astray, if possible, even the elect. See, I have told you beforehand. So, if they say to you, "Look, he is in the wilderness," do not go out. If they say, "Look, he is in the inner rooms,"

---

114 See chapter 4, "The Return of Christ," and chapter 5, "Satan's Little Season."

do not believe it. For as the lightning comes from the east and shines as far as the west, so will be the coming of the Son of Man. Wherever the corpse is, there the vultures will gather.

Jesus is telling the disciples, and us, how to recognize the true Messiah. When Jesus returns, we won't need to hear about it from someone else. We will see it ourselves. The time preceding the destruction of the temple was filled with false messiahs. Jesus said he will not show up to lead a rebellion, nor will he be someone who comes from obscurity, as he did in his first coming. He will come with blazing light. No one will miss it or debate if he really is the Messiah.

What does Jesus mean, though, by "Wherever the corpse is, there the vultures will gather"? The imagery is that of judgment.[115] In other words, Jesus said when he returns, he will return in judgment, not to lead a rebellion against Rome. The bottom line is Jesus is telling the disciples, those of that generation, and us, that the purpose of his return is judgment. Therefore, if you meet any other so-called messiahs, you can be sure they are false.

The Coming of the Son of Man

The next section, verses 29–35, moves us to the second coming of Christ. Remember, I pointed out at the beginning of this chapter that verses 4–35 deal primarily with the destruction of Jerusalem. However, this section contains a clear reference to the return of Christ; but we can't divorce it from its context.

Immediately after the tribulation of those days the sun will be darkened, and the moon will not give its light, and the stars will fall from heaven, and the powers of the heavens will be shaken. Then will appear in heaven the sign of the Son of Man, and then all the tribes of the earth will mourn, and they will see the Son of Man coming on the clouds of heaven with power and great glory. And he will send out his angels with a loud trumpet call, and they will gather his elect from the four winds, from one end of heaven to the other. From the fig tree learn its lesson: as soon as its branch becomes tender and puts out its leaves, you know that summer is near. So also, when you see all these things, you know that he is near, at the very gates. Truly, I say to you, this generation will not pass away until all these things take place. Heaven and earth will pass away, but my words will not pass away. (Matthew 24:29–35)

---

115 See Revelation 19:17–21 for similar judgment imagery.

Jesus just told the disciples what his second coming would look like, so they could ignore all the others who claimed to be the Messiah. When Jesus said, "After the tribulation of those days," he was referring to the tribulation that occurs before his second coming, which the tribulation at the time of the destruction of Jerusalem foreshadows. He uses the judgment imagery of the Old Testament, such as in chapters 13 and 34 of Isaiah, to describe his second coming:[116]

> Behold, the day of the LORD comes,
>   cruel, with wrath and fierce anger,
> to make the land a desolation
>   and to destroy its sinners from it.
> For the stars of the heavens and their constellations
>   will not give their light;
> the sun will be dark at its rising,
>   and the moon will not shed its light.
> I will punish the world for its evil,
>   and the wicked for their iniquity. (Isaiah 13:9–11a)

> All the host of heaven shall rot away,
>   and the skies roll up like a scroll.
> All their host shall fall,
>   as leaves fall from the vine,
>   like leaves falling from the fig tree. (Isaiah 34:4)

These prophecies from Isaiah refer to divine judgment against Babylon and Edom. "End of the world" language is used because it was the end for these nations. There was not a literal shaking of the heavens at these judgments, but these prefigure the final judgment, in which the Bible points to some type of physical change. We read this in 2 Peter 3:10:

> But the day of the Lord will come like a thief, and then the heavens will pass away with a roar, and the heavenly bodies will be burned up and dissolved, and the earth and the works that are done on it will be exposed.

---

116 Riddlebarger, *A Case for Amillennialism*, 201.

No signs in the sky provided an advance warning before the destruction of Jerusalem, so this can only be referring to the second coming of Christ in judgment. Again, remember the context. Jesus is telling the disciples, and their generation, how they can recognize all the false messiahs and false prophets. Jesus is telling us the same thing. There will be false prophets and false teachers throughout the gospel age.

The disciples asked, "What will be the sign of your coming?" Jesus answers in verse 30, "Then will appear in heaven the sign of the Son of Man." Jesus's physical return in the clouds is the sign we are looking for. There are two truths we see regarding the return of Christ. First, it will be obvious to all.[117] Verse 30 continues, "Then all the tribes of the earth will mourn, and they will see the Son of Man coming on the clouds of heaven with power and great glory." Everyone will see the return of Christ, which rules out any type of dispensational "secret" rapture. Second, his return is universal. The elect from every corner of the world will be gathered, and every nation will mourn.[118]

Jesus uses the lesson of the fig tree to teach that the generation who sees these signs will also see the fulfillment of the prophecy. Therefore, for the signs that apply to the destruction of Jerusalem, the generation that sees the signs will also see the destruction of Jerusalem. This is exactly what happened. Within a generation of Jesus's prophecy, Jerusalem was destroyed.

Furthermore, those who see these worldwide signs of intense tribulation, apostasy, and antichrist,[119] will be alive when Jesus returns. Jesus emphasized what he was saying was true when he said, "Heaven and earth will pass away, but my words will not pass away" (Matthew 24:35).

Predictions and Fulfillment

Based on the questions the disciples asked, the first section of the Olivet Discourse uses double fulfillment to describe both the destruction of the Jerusalem temple and the return of Christ. Below is a table that shows selected texts from verses 4–35, their fulfillment in AD 70, and their final fulfillment.[120]

---

117 See chapter 4, "The Return of Christ."
118 Doriani, *Matthew*, 378–79.
119 See chapter 5, "Satan's Little Season."
120 Taken from *Matthew*, vol. 2, Reformed Expository Commentary by Daniel M. Doriani. Copyright © 2008 by Daniel M. Doriani. Used by permission of HarperCollins Christian Publishing. www.harpercollinschristian.com.

Predictions and Text	Fulfillment by AD 70	Final Fulfillment
False christs will come (24:5, 23–24).	Jewish prophets predict God will deliver Jews from Rome.	The great Antichrist deceives many by his words and deeds.
Wars, famines, and earthquakes will strike (24:7–8).	Rome is often at war; there is famine in the reign of Claudius and there are major earthquakes.	The troubles of this life intensify near the end.
The gospel will be preached in the whole world (24:14).	The gospel is proclaimed throughout the known world.	The gospel is preached to every nation, language, and people.
The abomination that causes desolation will stand in the holy place (24:15).	Idolatrous Roman armies invade Jerusalem, fight and kill many, even in the temple.	Final rebellion against God brings religious abomination and desolation.
The sun and moon will be darkened when Jesus comes (24:29–31).	Jerusalem's fall foreshadows the end of earth's powers.	This world order ends when Christ returns.
The sign of the Son of Man will appear in heaven (24:30).	Fulfillment of prophecy shows Jesus reigns in heaven.	Jesus returns on clouds of the sky with angels.

Final Judgment

In the final section of Matthew 24:36–44, Jesus focused on answering the second question: "What will be the sign of your coming and of the end of the age?" Let's read his answer:

> But concerning that day and hour no one knows, not even the angels of heaven, nor the Son, but the Father only. For as were the days of Noah, so will be the coming of the Son of Man. For as in those days before the flood they were eating and drinking, marrying and giving in marriage, until the day when Noah entered the ark, and they were unaware until the flood came and swept them all away, so will be the coming of the Son of

Man. Then two men will be in the field; one will be taken and one left. Two women will be grinding at the mill; one will be taken and one left. Therefore, stay awake, for you do not know on what day your Lord is coming. But know this, that if the master of the house had known in what part of the night the thief was coming, he would have stayed awake and would not have let his house be broken into. Therefore you also must be ready, for the Son of Man is coming at an hour you do not expect.

There are a few notables in this section of the Olivet Discourse. First, Jesus speaks of "that day and hour." He is referring to the day of the Lord, the Day of Judgment. Remember what Jesus said in the Sermon on the Mount in Matthew 7:21–22:

Not everyone who says to me, "Lord, Lord," will enter the kingdom of heaven, but the one who does the will of my Father who is in heaven. On that day many will say to me, "Lord, Lord, did we not prophesy in your name, and cast out demons in your name, and do many mighty works in your name?"

Jesus said, "On that day many will say to me" (v. 22). To what day is he referring? The day of the final judgment. The context of the Olivet Discourse is judgment, so "that day and hour" refers to the Day of Judgment.

Next, we see Jesus emphasize there is no way to predict his coming in judgment. The disciples asked for a sign, and he told them his return is the sign. Then he said, "No one knows, not even the angels of heaven, nor the Son, but the Father only" (Matthew 24:36).

Jesus also uses the example of Noah to illustrate his point. In Noah's day, no one believed judgment was coming until it started to rain. Everyone could see the ark being built, and, according to Peter, Noah was a preacher of righteousness. Jesus also uses the picture of the two men in the field and the two women at the mill. One is taken away and the other is left behind. A few years ago, the *Left Behind* series of novels leaned into the popular notion that being left behind should be avoided at all costs. You should want to be taken away in the rapture.[121] But the Greek word translated as "take away" has overtones of violent action. Notice verse 39 says, "They were unaware until the flood came and swept them all away." It was those who were taken away that experienced judgment. Those

---

121 *Left Behind* is a series of novels by Tim LaHaye and Jerry Jenkins that presents in a fictionalized form the dispensational understanding of the return of Christ.

who were left behind on the earth experienced salvation. We do not want to be taken away in judgment; we want to be left behind for salvation.

Finally, the reason we are not given specific signs of the return of Jesus is so we may keep watch. Jesus compares his return to a thief in the night. Dispensationalists use this to argue for a secret rapture, but this has nothing to do with a secret return of Jesus. Jesus is simply pointing out that just as you do not know when a thief will break into your home, we do not know when Jesus will return. He said his return will be visible to all. It will not be secret so faithful disciples should always keep watch and be ready to welcome their returning King.[122]

Summary

The rest of chapters 24 and 25 continue with parables of the faithful and wise servant, the ten virgins, and the talents—parables about faithful servants who prepare for their master's return. Jesus ends his discourse with a description of the final judgment in Matthew 25:31–46.[123] The key takeaway is that we must look at this section of the Olivet Discourse in light of the questions asked by the disciples. Jesus assures them the temple will be destroyed and gives them the conditions that will exist at the time, but Jesus also corrects their idea that the destruction of the temple will signal his return and the end of the age. We cannot look at this passage as only applying to AD 70 or only applying to the future. Careful reading, along with understanding double fulfillment, is critical to a correct understanding of the Olivet Discourse and how it applies to eschatology.

---

122 Doriani, *Matthew*, 380–83.
123 See chapter 9, "The Final Judgment."

Chapter 13

THE SEVENTY WEEKS

I n chapter 4 I made a case for Christ returning only once, contrary to the dispensationalist view that Jesus will return twice—once to gather his saints in the air at the rapture and later accompanied by his saints as he descends bodily to earth at the end of the seven-year tribulation. This occurs before the millennium, the supposed one-thousand-year earthly reign of Christ. As we explored in chapter 7, a different but related perspective called historic premillennialism holds that Christ will return only once before the millennium.[124] Even though both premillennialist views are still popular, dispensational premillennialism is the more widespread of the two perspectives.

So, let's look at how dispensationalism's understanding of some of the events surrounding the return of Christ originated. Our focus in this chapter is the dispensational seven-year tribulation. One of the primary portions of Scripture dispensationalists use to establish their end times chronology is the "seventy weeks" passage from Daniel 9:24–27:

> Seventy weeks are decreed about your people and your holy city, to finish the transgression, to put an end to sin, and to atone for iniquity, to bring in everlasting righteousness, to seal both vision and prophet, and to anoint a most holy place. Know therefore and understand that from the going out of the word to restore and build Jerusalem to the coming of an anointed one, a prince, there shall be seven weeks. Then for sixty-two weeks it

---

124 See chapter 7, "The Millennium."

shall be built again with squares and moat, but in a troubled time. And after the sixty-two weeks, an anointed one shall be cut off and shall have nothing. And the people of the prince who is to come shall destroy the city and the sanctuary. Its end shall come with a flood, and to the end there shall be war. Desolations are decreed. And he shall make a strong covenant with many for one week, and for half of the week he shall put an end to sacrifice and offering. And on the wing of abominations shall come one who makes desolate, until the decreed end is poured out on the desolator.

This is an intriguing and mysterious passage, but it is critical to the dispensational end-times chronology. Kim Riddlebarger gives us the importance of this passage to the dispensationalist:

> The dispensational interpretation of Daniel 9:24–27 is one of the pillars of their entire system. From this passage, dispensationalists develop their doctrine of a future seven-year tribulation period, which commences when the Antichrist signs a peace treaty with the nation of Israel about the time of the secret rapture. Dispensationalists use this section of Daniel to set out what they perceive to be the future course of Israel's history and God's dealings with the Gentile nations. They teach that a "great parenthesis," also known as the church age, results from the supposed gap between the sixty-ninth and seventieth week of this prophecy.[125]

For the dispensationalist, the sequence of future events hinges on this passage, and much of their interpretation is driven by their separation of Israel and the Church. The dispensationalist Alva J. McClain (1888–1968) says that in the seventy weeks prophecy, "We have the indispensable chronological key to all New Testament prophecy." He goes on to say this passage gives us the interpretive grid needed to interpret the Olivet Discourse (Matthew 24–25) and most of Revelation. This passage is so important to the dispensationalist view that if you rebut their interpretation of the seventy weeks, their whole end-time system collapses.[126] The final week (or seven) of Daniel's prophecy includes the

---

125 Riddlebarger, *A Case for Amillennialism*, 177–78. Excerpt from *A Case for Amillennialism* by Kim Riddlebarger, copyright © 2013. Used by permission of Baker Books, a division of Baker Publishing Group.

126 Riddlebarger, *A Case for Amillennialism*, 178

rapture, the Antichrist, the seven-year tribulation, and the return of Christ before the millennium. Also, dispensationalism equates the seventieth week of Daniel to Revelation 6–19 since, according to the dispensationalist, these chapters describe the events that will occur during that week.

Seventy Sevens

Given the importance of this passage, let's see if their interpretation holds. The word translated *weeks* in most English translations of Daniel 9:24 means *sevens*. This term could mean seven days or seven years, but in chapter 9 of Daniel a *week* or *seven* means seven years; therefore, seventy weeks of years is 490 years.

Context

However, before we look at the meaning of this passage, let's understand the context. Daniel 9:4–19 records Daniel's prayer that God would restore Jerusalem and the temple. He prays this because, according to Daniel 9:1–3, he realizes the seventy years prophesied by Jeremiah have passed. Jeremiah prophesied that Judah would be in exile for seventy years due to her unfaithfulness (Jeremiah 25:8–14). In the prophecy, Jeremiah tells the people of Judah that destruction by the hands of Nebuchadnezzar is coming. They will be servants of the Chaldeans for seventy years after which God will punish Babylon. Chapter 29 of Jeremiah contains a letter the prophet wrote to the exiles. In verse 10 we read, "For thus says the LORD: When seventy years are completed for Babylon, I will visit you, and I will fulfill to you my promise and bring you back to this place." Daniel knows Jeremiah's prophecy, and because of this, he prays God would fulfill his promise. He prays a beautiful prayer of confession with a plea for mercy.

In addition, the theme of covenant is threaded throughout Daniel 9. Daniel appeals to God as the covenant God, and he confesses that God's people have broken the covenant. Furthermore, chapter 9 is the only chapter in Daniel that uses the covenant name Yahweh—and the prophet uses it six times.[127] The answer to the prayer is based on the number seven, which points to a covenantal sabbatical pattern, and the first period of weeks is forty-nine years, which points to the Year of Jubilee or Sabbath Year.[128] Daniel appeals to God to show mercy to his covenant people, and God responds in covenant language.

---

127 Meredith G. Kline, "The Covenant of the Seventieth Week," in *The Law and the Prophets: Old Testament Studies Prepared in Honor of Oswald Thompson Allis*, ed. John H. Skilton (Phillipsburg, NJ: Presbyterian & Reformed, 1974), 456.
128 Kline, "The Covenant of the Seventieth Week," 459.

In Daniel 9:20–23, the Lord sends the angel Gabriel to Daniel:

> While I was speaking and praying, confessing my sin and the sin of my people Israel, and presenting my plea before the LORD my God for the holy hill of my God, while I was speaking in prayer, the man Gabriel, whom I had seen in the vision at the first, came to me in swift flight at the time of the evening sacrifice. He made me understand, speaking with me and saying, "O Daniel, I have now come out to give you insight and understanding. At the beginning of your pleas for mercy a word went out, and I have come to tell it to you, for you are greatly loved. Therefore consider the word and understand the vision."

What follows is the prophecy concerning the seventy weeks (Daniel 9:24–27). This is God's answer to Daniel's prayer given through the angel Gabriel.

Week of Years

A week (or seven) is a week of years—that is, seven years. Why seven years? Why not seven days? From the beginning, God set aside the seventh day as a day of rest, and this was reaffirmed in the Mosaic covenant in the Ten Commandments. However, there was not just a seven-day pattern but also a seven-year pattern. This is seen in Leviticus 25:1–4:

> The LORD spoke to Moses on Mount Sinai, saying, "Speak to the people of Israel and say to them, When you come into the land that I give you, the land shall keep a Sabbath to the LORD. For six years you shall sow your field, and for six years you shall prune your vineyard and gather in its fruits, but in the seventh year there shall be a Sabbath of solemn rest for the land, a Sabbath to the LORD. You shall not sow your field or prune your vineyard."

Every seventh year, the land was to have a Sabbath rest. On top of that, after seven Sabbath years, which means after forty-nine years, the Year of Jubilee was to be proclaimed. This is in Leviticus 25:8–12:

> You shall count seven weeks of years, seven times seven years, so that the time of the seven weeks of years shall give you forty-nine years. Then you shall sound the loud trumpet on the tenth day of the seventh

month. On the Day of Atonement you shall sound the trumpet throughout all your land. And you shall consecrate the fiftieth year, and proclaim
liberty throughout the land to all its inhabitants. It shall be a jubilee for
you, when each of you shall return to his property and each of you shall
return to his clan. That fiftieth year shall be a jubilee for you; in it you shall
neither sow nor reap what grows of itself nor gather the grapes from the
undressed vines. For it is a jubilee. It shall be holy to you. You may eat
the produce of the field.

The Lord tells the Israelites to count seven weeks of years and explains this means
seven times seven years. In Leviticus, a week of years clearly means seven years. The year
after the forty-ninth year, the fiftieth year, is the Year of Jubilee. So based on Leviticus, the
seventy weeks in Daniel 9:24–27 is seventy weeks of years. Also, this means the seventy
weeks are ten Jubilees because seventy weeks of years is 490 years.[129] So, after the seventy
weeks, God will usher in the ultimate Jubilee.

How does this relate to the exile? Leviticus 26 gives the blessings for obedience and
curses for disobedience to the covenant. At the end of the curses in verses 43–45, God
describes the exile:

But the land shall be abandoned by them and enjoy its Sabbaths while it
lies desolate without them, and they shall make amends for their iniquity,
because they spurned my rules and their soul abhorred my statutes. Yet for
all that, when they are in the land of their enemies, I will not spurn them, neither will I abhor them so as to destroy them utterly and break my covenant
with them, for I am the LORD their God. But I will for their sake remember
the covenant with their forefathers, whom I brought out of the land of Egypt
in the sight of the nations, that I might be their God: I am the LORD.

According to Leviticus, exile to Babylon will be needed because the land must have the
Sabbaths that were ignored. This reason for the exile is also given in 2 Chronicles 36:20–21:

He [Nebuchadnezzar] took into exile in Babylon those who had escaped
from the sword, and they became servants to him and to his sons until
the establishment of the kingdom of Persia, to fulfill the word of the LORD

---

129 Riddlebarger, *A Case for Amillennialism*, 179.

> by the mouth of Jeremiah, until the land had enjoyed its Sabbaths. All the
> days that it lay desolate it kept Sabbath, to fulfill seventy years.

Daniel understands the seventy years of exile have been completed, and the land has enjoyed its Sabbaths, but the Lord introduces a new period, the seventy weeks. God takes the seventy years of the exile and multiplies it by seven. Four times in the curses for disobedience in Leviticus 26, the people are told God will multiply the curses sevenfold. Therefore, the exile is being extended until the problem of sin is permanently dealt with. Remember, when the people returned from exile, they were not a sovereign nation. Their initial return was not the ultimate promised restoration. So, God tells Daniel there will be a partial end to the current exile, but the exile is being continued until the final Jubilee.

Interpretation

Let's look closely at verses 24–27. Verse 24 says,

> Seventy weeks are decreed about your people and your holy city, to finish
> the transgression, to put an end to sin, and to atone for iniquity, to bring in
> everlasting righteousness, to seal both vision and prophet, and to anoint
> a most holy place.

New Covenant

The people had gone into exile because of their sin. Daniel knows the prophecies of Jeremiah, so he is looking for the new covenant prophesied by Jeremiah (Jeremiah 31:31–34). Surely this new covenant will be instituted when the people return from exile. Now God tells Daniel the new covenant will not begin when the exiles return from Babylon. The new covenant will happen after the seventy weeks are complete. Many take the 490 years to be literal 490 years, but the period is symbolic. In Matthew 18:21–22, Jesus answers a question from Simon Peter:

> Then Peter came up and said to him, "Lord, how often will my brother sin
> against me, and I forgive him? As many as seven times?" Jesus said to
> him, "I do not say to you seven times, but seventy-seven times."

Whereas the ESV has seventy-seven, many English translations have seventy times seven.[130] Jesus did not just pull seventy times seven out of thin air. He knew the significance

---

130 For example, KJV, NKJV, CSB, and LSB.

of seventy times seven—completeness or fullness. Jesus expanded Peter's understanding of forgiveness by showing Peter there is no limit to forgiveness. So, here in Daniel, Gabriel gives Daniel the complete picture of new covenant redemption. After seventy weeks of years, sin will be no more since it will have been atoned for, and there will be everlasting righteousness. The phrase "seal both vision and prophet" does not mean that vision and prophecy will be sealed so nobody has access to it. The idea of *sealing* here is ownership. Iain Duguid explains it like this:

> "Sealing" here does not so much indicate closing their books or keeping their words secret, but rather vindicating them, stamping them with God's seal of ownership through their fulfillment, just as a document might be sealed with the mark of its owner.[131]

"Anoint a most holy place" at the end of Daniel 9:24 refers to the temple. God says the destroyed temple in Jerusalem will be re-consecrated.[132] Some translations simply say, "anoint the most holy,"[133] which would refer to the anointing of the Messiah. All this language—finishing the transgression, putting an end to sin, atoning for iniquity, bringing in everlasting righteousness, sealing up vision and prophet, and anointing the most holy place—is all new covenant language. Finishing transgression, ending sin, and atoning for iniquity points to the passive obedience of Christ in his work on the cross, and bringing in everlasting righteousness points to the active obedience of Christ in his life of obedience. All of this relates to his priestly work. The sealing of vision and prophet relates to Christ's prophetic work, and the anointing of the Most Holy likely relates to Christ's kingly work.[134] The seventy weeks include not only the initiation of the new covenant but also its consummation.

Three Periods

Let's turn our attention to verse 25:

> Know therefore and understand that from the going out of the word to restore and build Jerusalem to the coming of an anointed one, a prince,

---

131 Iain M. Duguid, *Daniel*, Reformed Expository Commentary (Phillipsburg, NJ: P&R Publishing Co., 2008), 165. Reprinted from *Daniel* by Iain M. Duguid, copyright 2008, P&R Publishing, Phillipsburg, NJ.

132 Duguid, *Daniel*, 165.

133 For example, KJV and NKJV.

134 Riddlebarger, *A Case for Amillennialism*, 181.

> there shall be seven weeks. Then for sixty-two weeks it shall be built
> again with squares and moat, but in a troubled time.

The seventy weeks begins with the issuing of the decree to rebuild Jerusalem, which is recounted in 2 Chronicles 36:22–23:

> Now in the first year of Cyrus king of Persia, that the word of the LORD
> by the mouth of Jeremiah might be fulfilled, the LORD stirred up the spirit
> of Cyrus king of Persia, so that he made a proclamation throughout all his
> kingdom and also put it in writing: "Thus says Cyrus king of Persia, 'The
> LORD, the God of heaven, has given me all the kingdoms of the earth,
> and he has charged me to build him a house at Jerusalem, which is in
> Judah. Whoever is among you of all his people, may the LORD his God
> be with him. Let him go up.'"

With this decree by Cyrus, the seventy weeks of years begins. Daniel mentions three periods of weeks: seven weeks, sixty-two weeks, and then one week. During the first period of forty-nine years (seven weeks), the Jerusalem temple was rebuilt. However, during the next sixty-two weeks, trouble continues for Jerusalem. The end of Daniel 9:25 says, "Then for sixty-two weeks it shall be built again with squares and moat, but in a troubled time." This is the time between the completion of the second temple and the arrival of Jesus. This was the time of Antiochus IV Epiphanes, the pagan king mentioned previously who profaned the temple with idolatry and ceremonially unclean sacrifices and worship.

Seventieth Week

A great divide in interpretations comes in the understanding of the last week, the final seven years. Take a close look at Daniel 9:26:

> And after the sixty-two weeks, an anointed one shall be cut off and shall
> have nothing. And the people of the prince who is to come shall destroy
> the city and the sanctuary. Its end shall come with a flood, and to the end
> there shall be war. Desolations are decreed.

Most interpreters agree the *anointed one* who is cut off is Christ. This happened at the end of the sixty-nine weeks. According to dispensationalists, the church age began at that point, and the seventieth week was put on hold. This is called the great parenthesis. The church age, the time we are currently in, is a parenthesis or pause between the sixty-ninth and seventieth week. So, there is a gap lasting now over two thousand years between the sixty-ninth and seventieth week. The last week of years is the seven-year tribulation. Verse 26 speaks of the prince who is to come. According to dispensationalists, this is the Antichrist, who will bring trouble to the nation of Israel. Daniel 9:27 says,

> And he shall make a strong covenant with many for one week, and for half of the week he shall put an end to sacrifice and offering. And on the wing of abominations shall come one who makes desolate, until the decreed end is poured out on the desolator.

Based on this verse, dispensationalists say the Antichrist will make a peace treaty with the nation of Israel after the secret rapture of believers at the beginning of the last seven years. Then, after three and a half years, the Antichrist will break the treaty and end the sacrifices at the rebuilt temple. The Antichrist will then bring tribulation on the nation of Israel until Christ returns for the second time to establish his millennial kingdom. Dispensationalists hold to this interpretation because they interpret the *he* of verse 27 to refer to the prince of verse 26. Thus, it is the Antichrist who makes a strong covenant.

There are two errors here. The first is not recognizing the fulfillment of verse 24—the finishing transgression, ending sin, and so on—in the ministry of Jesus. Dispensationalists see this prophecy as applying only to the physical nation of Israel. They claim the events of verse 24 have yet to occur.[135]

The second error is applying a prophecy about Christ to the Antichrist. In the middle of the final seven, the "anointed one" puts an end to sacrifice and offering, and this is exactly what Jesus did when he suffered and died on the cross. Even though Jesus was cut off at the end of the sixty-ninth week, sacrifices and offerings ended in the middle of the seventieth week. This refers to the destruction of the temple by Titus in AD 70. In principle Christ put an end to the sacrificial system in his once-for-all sacrifice (Hebrews 9:26). However, the practice did not end until the destruction of the temple. As Hebrews 8:13 says, "In speaking of a new covenant, he makes the first one obsolete. And what is becoming obsolete and growing old is ready to vanish away." Eventually, the prince of the people, Titus, came and destroyed Jerusalem and the temple. Because dispensationalists do not primarily view the Scriptures from the

---

135 Riddlebarger, *A Case for Amillennialism*, 182.

perspective of the covenants, they miss that this whole passage in Daniel 9 is referring to the institution of the new covenant. Kim Riddlebarger gives us a helpful summary of the two dispensational errors:

> Dispensationalists insist that the subject of verse 27, "He will confirm a covenant with many for one seven," must refer back to the preceding *he*, that is, the ruler who would destroy the city and the sanctuary (v. 26). They, however, are in error, confusing the identity of the covenant maker, who is cut off for his people, with the Roman prince, i.e. antichrist. In order to make this fit into their interpretive scheme, dispensationalists insist that the Messiah is cut off after the sixty-two sevens. An indeterminate gap of time comes between the end of the sixty-nine sevens and the seventieth seven, they say, when the one who confirms a covenant with many (Israel) arrives on the scene to do his dastardly deed. The insertion of a gap of at least two thousand years between the sixty-ninth and seventieth week is a self-contradictory violation of the dispensationalist's professed literal hermeneutic. Where is the gap found in the text? Dispensationalists must insert it. The failure to acknowledge the obvious covenantal context of the messianic covenant maker of verse 27, who confirms a covenant with many, leads dispensationalists to confuse Christ with antichrist, A more serious interpretive error is hard to imagine.[136]

The last seven begins with the death of Christ—the anointed one is cut off. It ends when all that is prophesied in verse 24 is fully realized. Verse 27 says the anointed one makes a strong covenant with many. Thus, the last seven runs from the institution of the new covenant in the death of Christ to the consummation of the new covenant in the return of Christ. In the middle of the last week, there is an end to sacrifice and offering. Again, Christ accomplished this in principle at his death, but the practice ended officially when Titus destroyed Jerusalem in AD 70.

What about the last three and a half years though? What do they represent? The New Testament gives us the answer. In Revelation John refers to this as "a time, times, and half a time," as forty-two months, and as 1,260 days. For example, Revelation 12:1–6 says,

---

136 Riddlebarger, *A Case for Amillennialism*, 180–81. Excerpt from *A Case for Amillennialism* by Kim Riddlebarger, copyright © 2013. Used by permission of Baker Books, a division of Baker Publishing Group.

And a great sign appeared in heaven: a woman clothed with the sun, with the moon under her feet, and on her head a crown of twelve stars. She was pregnant and was crying out in birth pains and the agony of giving birth. And another sign appeared in heaven: behold, a great red dragon, with seven heads and ten horns, and on his heads seven diadems. His tail swept down a third of the stars of heaven and cast them to the earth. And the dragon stood before the woman who was about to give birth, so that when she bore her child he might devour it. She gave birth to a male child, one who is to rule all the nations with a rod of iron, but her child was caught up to God and to his throne, and the woman fled into the wilderness, where she has a place prepared by God, in which she is to be nourished for 1,260 days.

I addressed this in the chapter on Satan's little season.[137] The child born in Revelation 12:5 is Jesus, and the woman represents true Israel. This verse describes the time from Jesus's birth until his ascension. The woman, true Israel, or the Church, flees into the wilderness for 1260 days, which is three and a half years. This wilderness pilgrimage reminds us of the Israelites, who had been saved from slavery in Egypt but had not yet reached the Promised Land. Similarly, we have been saved from bondage to sin, but we are still in this world, looking toward a better country.

Revelation 12:7–12 describes the victory of Jesus over Satan on the cross:

Now war arose in heaven, Michael and his angels fighting against the dragon. And the dragon and his angels fought back, but he was defeated, and there was no longer any place for them in heaven. And the great dragon was thrown down, that ancient serpent, who is called the devil and Satan, the deceiver of the whole world—he was thrown down to the earth, and his angels were thrown down with him. And I heard a loud voice in heaven, saying, "Now the salvation and the power and the kingdom of our God and the authority of his Christ have come, for the accuser of our brothers has been thrown down, who accuses them day and night before our God. And they have conquered him by the blood of the Lamb and by the word of their testimony, for they loved not their lives even unto death. Therefore, rejoice, O heavens and you who dwell in them! But

---

137 See chapter 5, "Satan's Little Season."

woe to you, O earth and sea, for the devil has come down to you in great wrath, because he knows that his time is short!"

Even though Satan is defeated, he brings persecution to the people of God. They "loved not their lives even unto death," which refers to the perseverance of God's people despite persecution. The thought continues in verses 13 and 14:

And when the dragon saw that he had been thrown down to the earth, he pursued the woman who had given birth to the male child. But the woman was given the two wings of the great eagle so that she might fly from the serpent into the wilderness, to the place where she is to be nourished for a time, and times, and half a time.

Satan pursues the woman, which represents the Church. The Church, however, is flown into the wilderness where she is nourished for three and a half years. This is a picture of the church, enduring the wilderness of the world and trusting in the Lord until Jesus returns. The use of eagle imagery also points back to the exodus. Exodus 19:4 says, "You yourselves have seen what I did to the Egyptians, and how I bore you on eagles' wings and brought you to myself." God uses the imagery of eagles' wings to describe the deliverance of Israel from Egypt.[138] So, the picture in Revelation 12 shows us that God sustains and protects his church in the present age.

This 42-month period is also seen in Revelation 11 and 13. Meredith Kline (1922–2007) wrote,

It appears that the last half of the seventieth week is the age of the community of the new covenant, disengaged from the old covenant order with whose closing days its own beginnings overlapped for a generation. In the imagery of the New Testament Apocalypse, the last half week is the age of the church in the wilderness of the nations for a time, and times, and half a time (Rev. 12:14). Since the seventy weeks are ten jubilee eras that issue in the last jubilee, the seventieth week closes with angelic trumpeting of the earth's redemption and the glorious liberty of the children of God. The acceptable year of the Lord which came with Christ will then have fully come. Then the new Jerusalem whose temple is the Lord and the Lamb will

---

138 Also, see Isaiah 40:29–31.

descend from heaven (Rev. 21:10, 22) and the ark of the covenant will be seen (Rev. 11:19), the covenant the Lamb has made to prevail and the Lord has remembered.[139]

In other words, the three and a half years represent the time between the first and second comings of Christ. Therefore, the seventy weeks end at the consummation of all things when the final Jubilee begins. Iain Duguid writes,

> With the coming of Jesus into the world, and especially with his death and resurrection, the seventieth week has dawned. In Christ, our jubilee trumpet has sounded, and the victory over sin and transgression has been won. What is more, with the death of Jesus on the cross, the sacrifices of the Old Testament became redundant and worthless. The Son of Man gave his life as a ransom for the many, bringing those whom God had chosen into the new covenant relationship with the Lord (Mark 10:45). The new covenant of which Jeremiah spoke is now here, as our Lord himself taught us on the night before he died, when he called the cup that he shared with his disciples "the new covenant in my blood" (1 Cor. 11:25). With the coming of Christ, all of the things that Daniel 9:24 anticipated have been accomplished in principle; our sins are atoned for, our transgressions have been removed from us, and the words of the prophets have been vindicated. Of course, we still await the end of this seventieth week, the day when God will bring all of these things to final consummation: we still drink the cup of the new covenant time after time, proclaiming the Lord's death until he comes.[140]

What do we do, though, with the last part of Daniel 9:27, which says, "And on the wing of abominations shall come one who makes desolate, until the decreed end is poured out on the desolator"? This is difficult to translate and to interpret. It appears to be referring to the Antichrist. In his epistles, John tells us there will be many antichrists. But there will be a final manifestation of the Antichrist, what Paul calls the man of lawlessness. Daniel 9:27 refers to a final abomination that brings judgment. This fits what we know

---

139 Kline, "The Covenant of the Seventieth Week," 468–69.
140 Duguid, *Daniel*, 171–72. Reprinted from *Daniel* by Iain M. Duguid, copyright 2008, P&R Publishing, Phillipsburg, NJ.

concerning the man of lawlessness. So, there will be abominations that occur throughout the gospel age until the Antichrist brings the final abomination.[141] Iain Duguid understands this verse to refer to the rejection of Jesus by the people, which led to his crucifixion and the destruction of Jerusalem.[142] That fits the context. However, understanding this as referring to antichrists, the final Antichrist, and his destruction makes the most sense, given the reference to abominations, which is mentioned in Daniel 11 and 12 in reference to Antiochus and is referred to by Jesus in the Olivet Discourse. The meaning must be in line with the message of the New Testament.

Summary

There is no doubt that this is a difficult passage, but we cannot abandon our hermeneutics (principles of interpretation) when seeking to understand it. In line with most reformed Bible scholars, we should interpret this unclear passage in light of the clear teaching of the New Testament, and not vice versa. God sent Gabriel to tell Daniel he had a perfect plan to deal with the sin of the people, establish righteousness, vindicate his word, and establish a new temple. That was the Lord's announcement of the gospel given to Daniel.

---

141 See chapter 12, "The Olivet Discourse."
142 Duguid, *Daniel*, 173.

Chapter 14

EZEKIEL'S TEMPLE

In the previous chapter, we looked at the seventy weeks prophesied in chapter 9 of Daniel. According to dispensationalists, the last week (the seventieth week), is a seven-year tribulation period that occurs between the rapture of the Church and the bodily return of Christ to the earth. Dispensationalists believe this period deals primarily with the nation of Israel. One of the features of the dispensational interpretation of the seventy weeks of Daniel is that the Antichrist will put an end to the sacrifices occurring at the temple in Jerusalem.

Furthermore, dispensationalists believe that during the future seven-year tribulation, the Antichrist will be revealed, and he will make a peace treaty with Israel. After three and a half years, he will break the treaty and end temple sacrifices. He will set himself up as a god in the temple. Thus, according to the dispensational understanding, the existence of a physical temple with ongoing animal sacrifices is required for the timeline of the seventieth week.

However, most dispensational scholarship anticipates two future physical temples. At some point before the rapture, a temple will be rebuilt on the temple mount in Jerusalem. Currently, two mosques occupy those grounds. These will need to be razed, and a Jewish temple rebuilt so that Israel can reinstitute routine animal sacrifices on that site (until they are later stopped by the Antichrist). Some see this as the temple prophesied in chapters 40–48 of Ezekiel. However, most dispensationalists believe Ezekiel's temple will be built after the tribulation, during the millennial kingdom.

Let's consider the dispensationalist's claim that Old Testament temple worship will be reinstituted. Ezekiel prophesies about a great temple where sacrifices occur. The dispensational view of the restoration of temple worship comes from their commitment to a literal hermeneutic, their unyielding separation between Israel and the Church, and their refusal to interpret the Old Testament in light of the New Testament. So, what are we to make of these future temples? What are we to think of animal sacrifices happening again? We will look at an overview of Ezekiel's prophecy, but before we do, let's see what the New Testament says about the temple and the sacrifices.

The Temple

We know from reading and studying the Old Testament that the tabernacle, and later the temple, were central to Israelite worship. Exodus 25:8 says, "And let them make me a sanctuary, that I may dwell in their midst." The tabernacle and the temple were God's earthly sanctuary among his people. In Exodus 29:43–45 we read,

> There I will meet with the people of Israel, and it shall be sanctified by my glory. I will consecrate the tent of meeting and the altar. Aaron also and his sons I will consecrate to serve me as priests. I will dwell among the people of Israel and will be their God.

God will meet with his people at the tabernacle, so the tabernacle shows God dwells among his people.[143] The people of Israel are his people, and he is their God. When Solomon built the temple, he said in 1 Kings 8:13, "I have indeed built you an exalted house, a place for you to dwell in forever." So just like the tabernacle, the temple was God's house, where he dwelt with his people. The temple was also the way for the people to approach God. However, the Old Testament prophets predicted a time when the temple would no longer be necessary (Jeremiah 3:15–18; Malachi 1:10–11). Isaiah 2:2–3 prophesies of a time when there is a greater temple on a greater mountain:

> It shall come to pass in the latter days
> > that the mountain of the house of the LORD
> shall be established as the highest of the mountains,
> > and shall be lifted up above the hills;
> and all the nations shall flow to it,
> > and many peoples shall come, and say:
> "Come, let us go up to the mountain of the LORD,

---

143 Roderick Campbell, *Israel and the New Covenant* (Phillipsburg, NJ: Presbyterian and Reformed Publishing Company, 1954), 151.

to the house of the God of Jacob,
that he may teach us his ways
and that we may walk in his paths."
For out of Zion shall go forth the law,
and the word of the LORD from Jerusalem.

Isaiah was prophesying about our time.[144] As we noted back in chapter 2, the New Testament teaches that the latter days began with the death, burial, and resurrection of Jesus.[145] When Jesus was crucified, the curtain that separated the Holy Place from the Holy of Holies was torn in two from top to bottom (Matthew 27:50–51). The tearing of the curtain indicated no separation between God and his people. Also, the tearing of the curtain indicates the temple is no longer necessary because God's people now could approach him outside of that physical location. God dwells with his people through Jesus by the Holy Spirit. Hebrews 6:19–20 provides commentary on this:

> We have this as a sure and steadfast anchor of the soul, a hope that enters into the inner place behind the curtain, where Jesus has gone as a forerunner on our behalf, having become a high priest forever after the order of Melchizedek.

Jesus, as our high priest, has entered the true Holy of Holies, the true temple (Hebrews 9:24). He made atonement for us by the offering of his own blood, which secured for us an eternal redemption. If this redemption is eternal, it is also complete; nothing needs to be added to it. As Jesus said on the cross, "It is finished" (John 19:30).

Not only did Jesus enter the Holy of Holies on our behalf, but we now can enter the holy places through the blood of Jesus (Hebrews 10:19–20). There is a new curtain, the flesh of Jesus, through which we enter the true Holy of Holies. His death on the cross secured our entry into the very presence of God. We now enter the true temple through Jesus, not to offer animal sacrifices, but rather to offer spiritual sacrifices (1 Peter 2:4–5).

We are living stones that are part of a spiritual house, a holy priesthood before God through Christ. As Hebrews 13:15 says, our sacrifices are now sacrifices of thanksgiving and praise.[146] Paul tells us in Romans 12:1, "I appeal to you therefore, brothers, by the

---

144 Campbell, *Israel and the New Covenant*, 153–54.
145 See chapter 2, "The Last Days."
146 Campbell, *Israel and the New Covenant*, 151–52.

mercies of God, to present your bodies as a living sacrifice, holy and acceptable to God, which is your spiritual worship." Our sacrifices are no longer sacrifices for atonement, for Jesus was not only our high priest but also our once-for-all atoning sacrifice. The phrase "once for all" is used four times in Hebrews (Hebrews 7:27; 9:12, 26; 10:10). Let's look at Hebrews 9:11–12:

> But when Christ appeared as a high priest of the good things that have come, then through the greater and more perfect tent (not made with hands, that is, not of this creation) he entered once for all into the holy places, not by means of the blood of goats and calves but by means of his own blood, thus securing an eternal redemption.

Not only do we have access to God through the blood of Jesus, but by him the Church is being built up into the temple of God, as we see in Paul's letters:

> For through him we both have access in one Spirit to the Father. So then you are no longer strangers and aliens, but you are fellow citizens with the saints and members of the household of God, built on the foundation of the apostles and prophets, Christ Jesus himself being the cornerstone, in whom the whole structure, being joined together, grows into a holy temple in the Lord. In him you also are being built together into a dwelling place for God by the Spirit. (Ephesians 2:18–22)

> Do you not know that you are God's temple and that God's Spirit dwells in you? If anyone destroys God's temple, God will destroy him. For God's temple is holy, and you are that temple. (1 Corinthians 3:16–17)

So, we must approach any prophecy of a temple in the Old Testament with these things in mind: there will be a time when a physical temple will no longer be necessary; Jesus entered the true temple as high priest with his blood as the final sacrifice; and Christ's Church is the temple.

Tribulation Temple

Now let's go back to where we started with the dispensational claim of a millennial temple, in addition to the one desecrated during the seven-year tribulation. According to dispensationalists, the temple prophesied by Ezekiel is the millennial temple, but there also must be a temple during the tribulation. The primary evidence dispensationalists have for the temple that exists during their seven-year tribulation is their interpretation of Daniel 9:24–27, which we have noted is incorrect.[147] Dispensationalists also appeal to 2 Thessalonians 2:3–4 to prove the necessity of a new earthly temple:

> Let no one deceive you in any way. For that day will not come, unless the rebellion comes first, and the man of lawlessness is revealed, the son of destruction, who opposes and exalts himself against every so-called god or object of worship, so that he takes his seat in the temple of God, proclaiming himself to be God.

According to their interpretation, the man of lawlessness will take his seat in a literal temple in Jerusalem.[148] John Walvoord (1910–2002), one of the most prominent dispensationalists of the twentieth century, wrote,

> The scriptures indicate plainly that there will be a Temple built in the future in which Orthodox Jews will renew the ancient sacrifices prescribed by the Mosaic law. And the Temple will be built sometime before the world government takes over three and one half years before the second coming. And we're told in Daniel 9:27, as well as in other passages, that when that takes place, the Antichrist is going to stop the sacrifices and set the Temple up as a Temple for himself. We anticipate that that could be done soon; we don't know when the Temple will be built, we just know it is going to be in operation at that point when the sacrifices cease.[149]

However, since it is not the Antichrist who ends sacrifices and offerings at a rebuilt temple, but it is Jesus who ends them by his death on the cross, we cannot read this verse as evidence of a temple in Jerusalem when Jesus returns. Given that, let's turn our focus to the unique temple prophesied about in Ezekiel 40–48.

---

147 See chapter 13, "The Seventy Weeks."

148 Given the previous section showed that a physical temple is obsolete, "temple" in 2 Thessalonians 2:4 must reference the spiritual temple of the Church.

149 John F. Walvoord, in interview with Randall Price, San Marcos, TX, September 20, 1998, quoted in Randall Price, *The Coming Last Days Temple* (Eugene, OR: Harvest House Publishers, 1999), 251.

Millennium Temple

Based on what we have already seen in the New Testament, the idea of a literal temple with animal sacrifices cannot be correct. However, classic dispensationalism clings to their interpretation that a temple will be built, especially during the millennium. John Walvoord wrote this in his book *Israel in Prophecy*,

> A number of Scriptures also describe the temple worship which will characterize the millennial kingdom. According to Ezekiel, a magnificent temple will be built, and a system of priesthood and memorial sacrifices will be set up. Scholars have not all agreed as to the interpretation of this difficult portion of Ezekiel. Some have felt it impossible to have a system of animal sacrifices subsequent to the one sacrifice of Christ on the cross in the light of New Testament passages stating that the sacrifice of Christ makes other sacrifices unnecessary. Though varied explanations have been given for Ezekiel 40-48 which unfold these details, no satisfactory explanation has been made other than that it is a description of millennial worship. In any case, it is clear that the sacrifices are not expiatory, but merely memorials of the one complete sacrifice of Christ. If in the wisdom and sovereign pleasure of God the detailed system of sacrifices in the Old Testament were a suitable foreshadowing of that which would be accomplished by the death of His Son, and if a memorial of Christ's death is to be enacted, it would seem not unfitting that some sort of a sacrificial system would be used. While problems remain, it seems clear that Israel will have an ordered worship with Jerusalem once again the center of their religious as well as political life. A new order of priesthood would be required somewhat different than the Aaronic order, and rituals will be observed similar to the Mosaic order but differing in many aspects. In any case, a spiritual life of wonderful depth and reality far beyond anything Israel had known in their entire history will characterize her experience in the millennial kingdom.[150]

Walvoord suggests that the New Testament's presentation of the sacrifice of Christ as the final sacrifice does not rule out a future temple. Ezekiel prophesies a temple will be

---

150 John F. Walvoord, *Israel in Prophecy* (Grand Rapids, MI: Zondervan Publishing House, 1962), 125–26. Taken from *Israel in Prophecy* by John F. Walvoord Copyright © 1962 by John F. Walvoord. Used by permission of HarperCollins Christian Publishing. www.harpercollinschristian.com

built; therefore, this temple will be built, and animal sacrifices will be reinstituted with some type of new priesthood. He does acknowledge these sacrifices are only memorial in nature. However, notice that he arbitrarily assigns this temple to the millennium. Walvoord maintains that the only good explanation for Ezekiel's temple is that it will be used in worship during the millennium. However, there is no explicit or implicit link between Ezekiel 40–48 and Revelation 20.

Context

Before we look at the prophecy of the temple, let's understand the context. Ezekiel is in exile with his fellow Israelites who remember Jerusalem's magnificent temple. In chapter 10 Ezekiel described the glory of the Lord departing from it. In chapter 16 Ezekiel tells the people the exile is God's wrath against them because of their disobedience and idolatry. Further, we read this in Ezekiel 33:10,

> And you, son of man, say to the house of Israel, Thus have you said: "Surely our transgressions and our sins are upon us, and we rot away because of them. How then can we live?"

Because of their sin and idolatry, they are in exile, and Jerusalem is in ruins. They believe all hope is lost. The exiles ask, "How then can we live?" The Lord's promises seem hollow, and restoration is unlikely. However, God has not abandoned his people, and restoration will happen. How can God reaffirm the ultimate restoration of his people in terms that will be meaningful to them? A vision of a restored temple, city, and nation is what they needed.[151]

Description

In Ezekiel 40–48, we are shown a glimpse of a restored and reordered Israel through a series of very detailed descriptions of life in this idyllic setting. Ezekiel 40–42 give detailed measurements of a temple. Chapter 40 gives the measurements of the outer and inner courts, the north and south gates, the chambers for the priests, and the vestibule. Chapter 41 specifies the measurements of the Holy of Holies along with structures built into the walls. Then in chapter 42, various chambers of the temple are described.

Chapter 43 describes the glory of God filling the temple with the latter half of the chapter describing the altar and the sacrifices required. In chapter 44 Ezekiel sees the east

---

151 "Ezekiel Sees a New Temple," *Tabletalk* 37, no. 10 (October 2013): 40.

gate, which is shut, and it will remain shut. Only a prince can use this gate, not for access, though, but rather for sharing a fellowship meal before the Lord.[152] Also in chapter 44, temple rules are instituted; no uncircumcised foreigners shall enter the temple, and the Levitical priests must follow certain purity codes to perform their duties.

Chapter 45 marks off the land for the temple and describes additional offerings and festivals, while chapter 46 reveals guidelines for how everyone from the prince to the common Israelite must conduct themselves in worship. In chapter 47, though, something unusual happens. Water flows from the inner sanctuary to the south of the altar and then out the east gate. The water starts as a trickle but becomes a mighty river. Then, beginning in verse 13 of chapter 47 and carrying through the end of the book, the Lord gives the boundaries for the land. He first gives the boundaries of Israel, then the boundaries for each of the twelve tribes of Israel, and finally the boundaries of the new city.[153]

Interpretation

As we look at Ezekiel 40–48 as a whole and consider what all this means, the debate is whether Ezekiel's vision of a temple is descriptive or prescriptive. The dispensationalist view says the vision is prescriptive in that it lays out how the temple must be built and the sacrifices that must be reinstituted. However, I submit the vision is in fact descriptive. Visions in the Bible do not usually give us *direction*. Rather, they give us *insight* into God's working now and in the future.

Sacrifices

Let's consider the sacrifices that occur in the temple, as described in Ezekiel 45:13–20:

> This is the offering that you shall make: one sixth of an ephah from each homer of wheat, and one sixth of an ephah from each homer of barley, and as the fixed portion of oil, measured in baths, one tenth of a bath from each cor (the cor, like the homer, contains ten baths). And one sheep from every flock of two hundred, from the watering places of Israel for grain offering, burnt offering, and peace offerings, to *make atonement* for them, declares the Lord GOD. All the people of the land shall be obliged to give this offering to the prince in Israel. It

---

152 David J. Reimer, study note on Ezekiel 44:1–3 in *The ESV Study Bible* (Wheaton, IL: Crossway, 2008), 1572.
153 Reimer, *ESV Study Bible*, 1577.

shall be the prince's duty to furnish the burnt offerings, grain offerings, and drink offerings, at the feasts, the new moons, and the Sabbaths, all the appointed feasts of the house of Israel: he shall provide the sin offerings, grain offerings, burnt offerings, and peace offerings, to *make atonement* on behalf of the house of Israel. Thus says the Lord GOD: In the first month, on the first day of the month, you shall take a bull from the herd without blemish, and purify the sanctuary. The priest shall take some of the blood of the sin offering and put it on the doorposts of the temple, the four corners of the ledge of the altar, and the posts of the gate of the inner court. You shall do the same on the seventh day of the month for anyone who has sinned through error or ignorance; so you shall *make atonement* for the temple.

Notice three times sacrifices and offerings are said to *make atonement*. Remember that dispensationalism teaches the sacrifices at the millennial temple are memorial in nature; that is, they look back to the sacrifice of Christ. However, memorial sacrifices are not found in Ezekiel. The sacrifices and offerings in Ezekiel are said to *make atonement*. If we are to understand this vision as prescriptive, then we have a stark contradiction with the teaching of the New Testament, which says the sacrifice of Christ on the cross was the final atoning sacrifice.

Another view of these sacrifices is held by dispensationalist Randall Price. He suggests that if Ezekiel says these offerings make atonement, then they must, in some sense, make atonement. His argument equates the sacrifices of the Ezekiel temple with the Old Testament sacrifices. Even though the Old Testament sacrifices made atonement, they did not make final atonement. Therefore, these reinstituted sacrifices do not replace the sacrifice of Christ, but rather they only make a provisional atonement in the same way as the Old Testament sacrifices.[154] This still misses the point, though, that the sacrifice of Christ was the final, complete, and efficacious sacrifice.

The sacrificial system of the Old Testament served the covenantal relationship between God and Israel. Sacrifice provided the way to restore the covenant relationship by offering a substitute as a ransom payment. It was a tribute payment from the subjects to the king. It was a way for the subjects to have a covenant meal with their king, and it was the way for the king to dwell with his subjects since the sacrifices cleansed impurity. All these sacrificial functions find their fulfillment in Christ. Jesus atones for us; he pays our

---

154 Price, *The Coming Last Days Temple*, 556–57.

tribute; through him, we have fellowship with the Father; and he is the one who cleanses us and the heavenly temple on our behalf.[155] Keith Mathison says it like this:

> It is impossible to interpret Ezekiel 40–48 in a strictly literal manner in reference to a future millennium without denying the clear teaching of Hebrews on the final sacrifice of Christ. To do so introduces a contradiction into Scripture that is easily avoided by seeing Ezekiel's descriptions as figurative. If the Old Testament prophets could prophesy about Christ figuratively in terms of the Levitical sacrifices, why could Ezekiel not have "prophesied the church age [figuratively] in terms of the Old Testament religious system with which ancient Israel was familiar?" Jesus did not come as a literal lamb with four legs and wool, and neither will a future millennium come with literal bloody sacrifices. Dispensationalists cannot be consistently literal in their interpretation of this passage. That would demand the restoration of bloody, atoning (not memorial) animal sacrifices, which is impossible now that Christ has offered himself as the final sacrifice.[156]

Ezekiel says the sacrifices at this temple make atonement; thus, what Ezekiel describes cannot be prescriptive. God is giving his people a message, not a command.

Water

Also, consider the water that proceeds from the temple. What does the New Testament say about water? Look at John 4:7–14, where we read about Jesus with the Samaritan woman:

> A woman from Samaria came to draw water. Jesus said to her, "Give me a drink." (For his disciples had gone away into the city to buy food.) The Samaritan woman said to him, "How is it that you, a Jew, ask for a drink from me, a woman of Samaria?" (For Jews have no dealings with Samaritans.) Jesus answered her, "If you knew the gift of God, and who it is that is saying to you, 'Give me a drink,' you would have asked him, and

---

155 Iain M. Duguid, *Ezekiel*, The NIV Application Commentary (Grand Rapids, MI: Zondervan, 1999), 524–25.

156 Keith Mathison, *Dispensationalism: Rightly Dividing the People of God?* (Phillipsburg, NJ: P&R Publishing, 1995), 8. Reprinted from *Dispensationalism: Rightly Dividing the People of God?* by Keith Mathison, copyright 1995, P&R Publishing, Phillipsburg, NJ.

he would have given you living water." The woman said to him, "Sir, you have nothing to draw water with, and the well is deep. Where do you get that living water? Are you greater than our father Jacob? He gave us the well and drank from it himself, as did his sons and his livestock." Jesus said to her, "Everyone who drinks of this water will be thirsty again, but whoever drinks of the water that I will give him will never be thirsty again. The water that I will give him will become in him a spring of water welling up to eternal life."

Jesus offers the woman water from a well that will never run dry. Furthermore, the water of the Spirit brings eternal life. This is confirmed in John 7:37–39:

On the last day of the feast, the great day, Jesus stood up and cried out, "If anyone thirsts, let him come to me and drink. Whoever believes in me, as the Scripture has said, 'Out of his heart will flow rivers of living water.'" Now this he said about the Spirit, whom those who believed in him were to receive, for as yet the Spirit had not been given, because Jesus was not yet glorified.

So, what is the result of the water coming from the temple? Ezekiel 47:6–12 picks up right after the river has been described:

And he said to me, "Son of man, have you seen this?" Then he led me back to the bank of the river. As I went back, I saw on the bank of the river very many trees on the one side and on the other. And he said to me, "This water flows toward the eastern region and goes down into the Arabah, and enters the sea; when the water flows into the sea, the water will become fresh. And wherever the river goes, every living creature that swarms will live, and there will be very many fish. For this water goes there, that the waters of the sea may become fresh; so everything will live where the river goes. Fishermen will stand beside the sea. From Engedi to Eneglaim it will be a place for the spreading of nets. Its fish will be of very many kinds, like the fish of the Great Sea. But its swamps and marshes will not become fresh; they are to be left for salt. And on the banks, on both sides of the river, there will grow all kinds of trees for food. Their leaves will not wither, nor their fruit fail, but they will bear fresh fruit every month, because the water for them flows from the sanctuary. Their fruit will be for food, and their leaves for healing."

This water brings life. There are trees on the banks of the river, and the water makes salt water fresh. Furthermore, the trees never wither, and they produce fruit every month, and the leaves of the trees bring healing. This river brings unending life. Compare this with Revelation 22:1–2:

Then the angel showed me the river of the water of life, bright as crystal, flowing from the throne of God and of the Lamb through the middle of the street of the city; also, on either side of the river, the tree of life with its twelve kinds of fruit, yielding its fruit each month. The leaves of the tree were for the healing of the nations.

Revelation 22:1–2 is included in the description of the New Jerusalem in the new heavens and new earth. Notice the tree of life is on both sides of the river of the water of life. It produces fruit each month, and the leaves are for the healing of the nations. This is very similar to the description in Ezekiel 47:12.

The very last verse of Ezekiel says, "And the name of the city from that time on shall be, The LORD Is There" (Ezekiel 48:35). In other words, the city is the temple, the place of God's presence. Revelation 21:22 says of the New Jerusalem, "And I saw no temple in the city, for its temple is the Lord God the Almighty and the Lamb." Furthermore, Revelation 22:3–5 says,

No longer will there be anything accursed, but the throne of God and of the Lamb will be in it, and his servants will worship him. They will see his face, and his name will be on their foreheads. And night will be no more. They will need no light of lamp or sun, for the Lord God will be their light, and they will reign forever and ever.

Revelation is describing the ultimate fulfillment of Ezekiel's temple vision. The throne of God in Revelation 22:1 equates to the temple described by Ezekiel. To the Old Testament saints, the temple was the throne of God, so God gave them a picture of a magnificent temple where he would dwell with his people. If we look for a literal temple to be built, we miss the message of Ezekiel's temple; therefore, we should not expect an earthly temple to be built in the future.

Summary

Briefly, there are other reasons why the temple cannot be literal. First, Ezekiel 40:2 says the temple is on a very high mountain, and the temple mount in Jerusalem does not qualify as a very high mountain. This reminds us of what we read earlier in Isaiah 2:2:

> It shall come to pass in the latter days
>> that the mountain of the house of the LORD
> shall be established as the highest of the mountains,
>> and shall be lifted up above the hills;
> and all the nations shall flow to it.

Second, God says in Ezekiel 43:7 that he will dwell here among his people forever, not just one thousand years. Third, no instructions are given concerning the height or the construction materials. Remember, God gave specific dimensions for the tabernacle and specified the materials for the tabernacle. Finally, nowhere in these chapters does God command the people to build this temple.[157] Concerning these last two points Iain Duguid says,

> The absence of specified building materials is a particular problem for literal interpretation, since these are precisely described in other situations where God instructs his servants to construct such edifices as the tabernacle and Solomon's temple. Of course, it should also be noted that Ezekiel is not instructed to build anything, he merely has to observe and recount to his fellow exiles what he has seen. The building he sees is already in existence.[158]

I pointed out when we began our look at the interpretation of Ezekiel 40–48 that the debate is whether Ezekiel's vision of a temple is descriptive or prescriptive. The dispensationalist says the vision is prescriptive; therefore, the temple must be built, and the sacrifices reinstituted. However, given the teaching of the New Testament, we cannot take the vision of the temple in Ezekiel as prescriptive; therefore, it must be descriptive.

Ezekiel gives a vision, not legislation. There is certainly legislation in the vision, but we have vision in the form of legislation, not legislation in the form of vision. The Jews

---

157 Duguid, *Ezekiel*, 479n26.
158 Duguid, *Ezekiel*, 479. Taken from *Ezekiel* by Iain M. Duguid Copyright © 1999 by Iain M. Duguid. Used by permission of HarperCollins Christian Publishing. www. harpercollinschristian.com.

did not understand this vision as prescriptive and did not attempt to build this temple after the exile. The temple vision was meant to encourage repentance, faithful endurance, and hope for the future.[159] Therefore, we should not expect a temple to be rebuilt before Christ returns. The vision of the temple in Ezekiel points us to the New Jerusalem, where all who belong to Christ dwell with him face to face.

---

159 Duguid, *Ezekiel*, 523.

About the Author

Michael Carpenter has been an elder at Reformation Christian Fellowship in Newport News, VA for over twelve years. He oversees theological education and has written courses for the church on various topics such as eschatology, the person and work of Christ, the atonement, and understanding the Bible. Michael has been married for thirty-seven years to his wife and they have three children and six grandchildren. He can be reached at reformedandtransformed.com.

Appendix A

END TIMES CHARTS

I have covered a lot of ground, and it is easy to get lost. Typically, when studying eschatology, end-time charts are prevalent. So here I include charts that summarize each of the millennial views. These charts include many of the topics I covered.

Historic Premillennialism

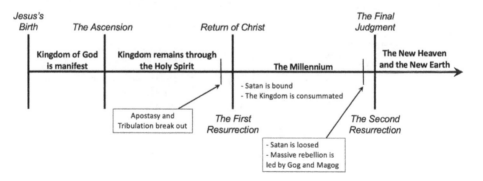

The first event is Jesus's birth, then the ascension after his death and resurrection. Between the ascension and the return of Christ, God rules his kingdom through the Holy Spirit. Sometime before Jesus returns, there is apostasy and tribulation. This is the time of the man of lawlessness. After the tribulation, Jesus returns and believers are resurrected. Then the millennium begins. Jesus reigns on the earth from a throne in Jerusalem. Both Jews and Gentiles constitute the people of God. During this period, Satan is bound, so evil is restrained but not eliminated. It will be a period of universal peace and prosperity among the nations, even though sin still exists. At the end of the millennium, Satan is released, and he leads a rebellion. Jesus crushes the rebellion, unbelievers are resurrected, and the great white throne judgment occurs. Following that is the new heavens and new earth.[160]

Dispensational Premillennialism

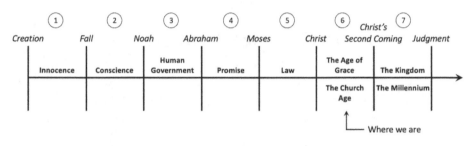

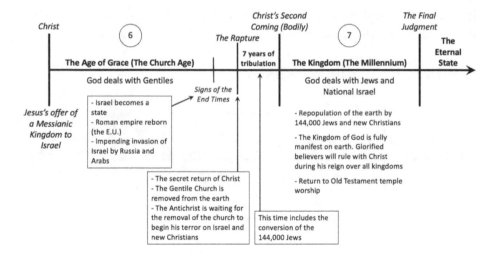

This diagram has two parts. The top diagram shows the seven dispensations. The bottom diagram expands on the dispensations of the Church Age and the Kingdom Age, which is the millennium. The Church Age is the period between the first coming of Christ and the rapture of the church. Before the rapture, Israel becomes a nation again, and the Roman empire is revived under the auspices of the European Union. Eventually, Israel is invaded by Russia and the Arab nations. All these signs indicate the rapture is imminent. Jesus then returns secretly and removes

---

160 Historic Premillennialism chart from Riddlebarger, *A Case for Amillennialism*, 43.
   Excerpt from *A Case for Amillennialism* by Kim Riddlebarger, copyright © 2013. Used by permission of Baker Books, a division of Baker Publishing Group.

the Church (the rapture). Believers are raised from the dead, and those alive at that time meet Jesus in the air and ascend into heaven with Jesus. The believers are judged at the judgment seat of Christ. Because the Church is absent from earth, so is the Holy Spirit. Nothing exists on earth to restrain the Antichrist. He begins seven years of persecution and tribulation against Israel. During this time, 144,000 Jews (possibly more) and other Gentiles are converted to Christianity. At the end of the seven years, Jesus returns bodily with his glorified saints, destroys the Antichrist, and establishes his millennial kingdom. Satan is bound, and Jesus, with his glorified saints, reigns from a throne in Jerusalem over the Jewish Christians and all those who survived the seven-year tribulation. The earth is occupied by both those in glorified bodies and those in perishable bodies. The temple is rebuilt, and the sacrifices are reinstituted, but these sacrifices look backward to the sacrifice of Christ (as opposed to the forward-looking sacrifices of the Old Testament). All the unfulfilled Old Testament prophecies are realized during the millennium. At the end of the millennium, which is exactly one thousand years, Satan is released and gathers the nations for battle. Jesus crushes the rebellion, and unbelievers are resurrected and judged at the great white throne judgment. The final state then begins. Classic dispensationalism believes Israel will remain on the new earth, and the Church will be in heaven. Progressive dispensationalists see Jew and Gentile together as one on the new earth.[161]

Postmillennialism

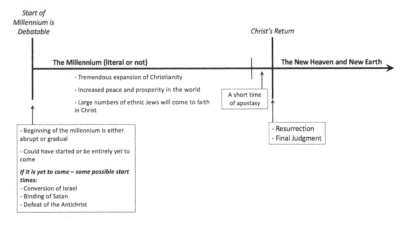

According to postmillennialism, when the millennium begins and how long it lasts are uncertain. As the gospel continues to spread, the world is transformed into a place with

---

161 Dispensational Premillennialism chart from Riddlebarger, *A Case for Amillennialism*, 42. Excerpt from *A Case for Amillennialism* by Kim Riddlebarger, copyright © 2013. Used by permission of Baker Books, a division of Baker Publishing Group.

less evil and more righteousness. Whereas all other millennial views see conditions getting worse as we approach the return of Christ, postmillennialism sees the world improving. The millennium may have already started, or it still may be in the future. If it is still in the future, its start could be signaled by a mass conversion of Jews, the binding of Satan, or the defeat of the Antichrist. During the millennium, Christianity is predominant throughout the world, and there is peace and prosperity. Not all are true Christians, though. At the end of the millennium, Satan is released and gathers the nations for battle. Jesus returns for the one and only time and crushes the rebellion. All people, saved and unsaved, are resurrected and stand in judgment. Then the new heavens and new earth are established.[162]

Amillennialism

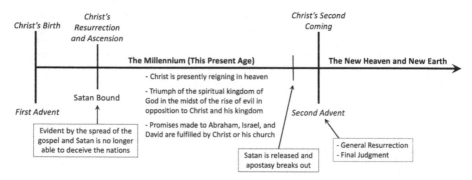

Satan is bound as a result of the death, resurrection, and ascension of Christ. That Satan is bound, does not mean he is absent or powerless. It means Satan cannot stop the spread of the gospel. Because Satan is bound, the millennium has already begun and is already longer than one thousand years. The millennium is another name for the present church age. Christ is reigning in heaven, and his kingdom is expanding through the spread of the gospel by the power of the Holy Spirit. All the Old Testament promises are fulfilled through Christ and his church. At some point before the return of Christ, Satan is released. When Satan is released, he will consolidate the nations in opposition to the Church and bring great tribulation to God's people. This will be the time of the man of lawlessness. When the tribulation is at its worst and the nations are united against the Church, Jesus will return and destroy all evil. All people are resurrected and stand before the great white throne for judgment. The sheep are separated from the goats (Matthew

---

162 Postmillennialism chart from Riddlebarger, *A Case for Amillennialism*, 44. Excerpt from *A Case for Amillennialism* by Kim Riddlebarger, copyright © 2013. Used by permission of Baker Books, a division of Baker Publishing Group.

25:32). The wicked are sent to the lake of fire with Satan, his demons, death, and Hades. Those who have their names in the book of life live forever with Jesus on the new earth.[163]

Notice the simplicity of amillennialism. There are not different events for different groups of people. Jesus returns once, and, when he returns, everyone is resurrected, the final judgment takes place, and the eternal state begins. However, we shouldn't believe amillennialism is correct just because it is simple. Rather, we can have confidence that amillennialism is also the most accurate way to account for and interpret the Scriptural passages that look forward to the return of Christ.

---

163 Amillennialism chart from Riddlebarger, *A Case for Amillennialism*, 45. Excerpt from *A Case for Amillennialism* by Kim Riddlebarger, copyright © 2013. Used by permission of Baker Books, a division of Baker Publishing Group.

Appendix B

FOR FURTHER STUDY

Here are some book recommendations for further study. These books have been especially helpful to me, and I have referenced most of them in this volume.

Eschatology

- *The Bible on the Life Hereafter* by William Hendriksen. This is a great starting book as it has short chapters with many Scripture references and questions to consider.
- *The Future of Everything* by William Boekstein. This is an easy read that covers individual and general eschatology with study questions for each chapter.
- *The Bible and the Future* by Anthony Hoekema.
- *The Promise of the Future* by Cornelis Venema. These last two books are more in-depth and give good explanations of the differences between a dispensational and covenantal approach to eschatology.

Revelation

- *More Than Conquerors* by William Hendriksen. This book is a great introduction to understanding Revelation. It is a classic book on Revelation and is easy to read. I recommend it to everyone.
- *Triumph of the Lamb* by Dennis E. Johnson. An excellent commentary on Revelation that presents a more nuanced structure of Revelation.

Amillennialism

- *A Case for Amillennialism* by Kim Riddlebarger. This book gives a sound defense for amillennialism while pointing out the problems with preterism, premillennialism, and postmillennialism. I recommend this book as the next step in the study of amillennialism.
- *Kingdom Come* by Sam Storms. This is one of the most comprehensive books of a reasonable size that presents the case for amillennialism. Since Sam Storms is a former dispensationalist, he presents the differences between dispensational premillennialism and amillennialism. I highly recommend this book.
- *The High King of Heaven* by Dean Davis. This book goes into great detail in presenting amillennialism. Davis shows how the Old Testament prophecies are fulfilled in Christ and examines the dispensational view in detail.

Dispensationalism

- *Dispensationalism: Rightly Dividing the People of God?* by Keith Mathison. This is a short, easy-to-read book that presents the major problems with dispensationalism.
- *Wrongly Dividing the Word of Truth: A Critique of Dispensationalism* by John Gerstner. This book is more academic and gives a brief history of dispensationalism, looks at the philosophy and hermeneutics of dispensationalism, and examines the theology of dispensationalism.

Israel and the Church

- *Israel and the New Covenant* by Roderick Campbell.
- *The Israel of God* by O. Palmer Robertson.

BIBLIOGRAPHY

Ascol, Tom. *The Perils and Promises of Christian Nationalism*. Cape Coral, FL: Founders Press, 2023.

Beale, G. K. *The Book of Revelation*. The New International Greek Testament Commentary. Grand Rapids, MI: Wm. B. Eerdmans Publishing Co., 1999, 2013.

Boettner, Loraine. "Postmillennialism." In *The Meaning of the Millennium: Four Views*, edited by Robert G. Clouse, 117–141. Downers Grove, IL: InterVarsity Press, 1977.

Campbell, Roderick. *Israel and the New Covenant*. Phillipsburg, NJ: Presbyterian and Reformed Publishing Company, 1954.

Chilton, David. *Productive Christians in an Age of Guilt Manipulators*. Tyler, TX: Institute for Christian Economics, 1981.

Davis, Dean. *The High King of Heaven*. Enumclaw, WA: Redemption Press, 2014.

Doriani, Daniel M. *Matthew*. Vol. 2. Reformed Expository Commentary. Phillipsburg, NJ: P&R, 2008.

Duguid, Iain M. *Daniel*. Reformed Expository Commentary. Phillipsburg, NJ: P&R, 2008.

Duguid, Iain M. *Ezekiel*. The NIV Application Commentary. Grand Rapids, MI: Zondervan, 1999.

"Ezekiel Sees a New Temple." *Tabletalk* 37, no. 10 (October 2013): 40.

Hendriksen, William. *More Than Conquerors*. Grand Rapids, MI: Baker Books, 1940, 1967, 1998.

Hendriksen, William. *The Bible on the Life Hereafter*. Grand Rapids, MI: Baker Book House, 1959.

Hendriksen, William. *The Gospel of Matthew*. New Testament Commentary. Grand Rapids, MI: Baker Book House, 1973.

Hoekema, Anthony A. *The Bible and the Future*. Grand Rapids, MI: Wm. B. Eerdmans Publishing Company, 1979.

"Introduction to The Revelation to John." In *The ESV Study Bible*, 2453–2462. Wheaton, IL: Crossway, 2008.

Kistemaker, Simon J. *Exposition of the Book of Revelation*. New Testament Commentary. Grand Rapids, MI: Baker Academic, 2001.

Kistemaker, Simon J. *Exposition of the First Epistle to the Corinthians*. New Testament Commentary. Grand Rapids, MI: Baker Books, 1993.

Kline, Meredith G. "The Covenant of the Seventieth Week." In *The Law and the Prophets: Old Testament Studies Prepared in Honor of Oswald Thompson Allis*, edited by John H. Skilton, 452–469. Phillipsburg, NJ: Presbyterian & Reformed, 1974.

Kreider, Glenn R. "What Is Dispensationalism? A Proposal." In *Dispensationalism and the History of Redemption*, edited by D. Jeffrey Bingham and Glenn R. Kreider, 15–46. Chicago: Moody Publishers, 2015.

Ladd, George Eldon. "Historic Premillennialism." In *The Meaning of the Millennium: Four Views*, edited by Robert G. Clouse, 17–40. Downers Grove, IL: InterVarsity Press, 1977.

Mathison, Keith A. *Dispensationalism: Rightly Dividing the People of God?* Phillipsburg, NJ: P&R Publishing, 1995.

Mathison, Keith A. *Postmillennialism: An Eschatology of Hope*. Phillipsburg, NJ: P&R Publishing, 1999.

Price, Randall. *The Coming Last Days Temple*. Eugene, OR: Harvest House Publishers, 1999.

Reimer, David J. Study notes on Ezekiel. In *The ESV Study Bible*, 1502–1580. Wheaton, IL: Crossway, 2008.

Riddlebarger, Kim. *A Case for Amillennialism: Understanding the End Times*. Expanded Edition. Grand Rapids, MI: Baker Books, 2003, 2013.

Ryrie, Charles C. *Dispensationalism Today*. Chicago: Moody Press, 1965.

Ryrie, Charles C. "A Synopsis of Bible Doctrine." In *Ryrie Study Bible*, 2055–2077. Chicago: Moody Press, 1995.

Snoeberger, Mark A. "Traditional Dispensationalism." In *Covenantal and Dispensational Theologies: Four Views on the Continuity of Scripture*, edited by Brent E. Parker and Richard J. Lucas, 147–182. Downers Grove, IL: InterVarsity Press, 2022.

Storms, Sam. *Kingdom Come: The Amillennial Alternative*. Fearn, Scotland: Christian Focus Publications, 2013.

Study notes on Isaiah. In *The Reformation Study Bible*, 1120-1250. Sanford, FL: Reformation Trust Publishing, 2015.

"The Day of the Lord in the Prophets." In *The ESV Study Bible*. 1668. Wheaton, IL: Crossway, 2008.

"The Plan of the Ages: Are We in the Last Days?" In *The Spirit of the Reformation Study Bible*. Ed. Pratt, Richard L. Jr., 1988–1989. Grand Rapids, MI: Zondervan, 2003.

Venema, Cornelis P. *The Bible and the Future*. Carlisle, PA: The Banner of Truth Trust, 2000.

Walvoord, John F. *Israel in Prophecy*. Grand Rapids, MI: Zondervan Publishing House, 1962.

A free ebook edition is available with the purchase of this book.

To claim your free ebook edition:

1. Visit MorganJamesBOGO.com
2. Sign your name CLEARLY in the space
3. Complete the form and submit a photo of the entire copyright page
4. You or your friend can download the ebook to your preferred device

Print & Digital Together Forever.

Snap a photo

Free ebook

Read anywhere